Microsoft .NET Framework 4.5 Quickstart Cookbook

Get up to date with the exciting new features in .NET 4.5
Framework with these simple but incredibly effective recipes

Jose Luis Latorre Millas

[PACKT] enterprise

professional expertise distilled

PUBLISHING

BIRMINGHAM - MUMBAI

Microsoft .NET Framework 4.5 Quickstart Cookbook

First published: May 2013

Production Reference: 1160513

Published by Packt Publishing Ltd.
Livery Place
35 Livery Street
Birmingham B3 2PB, UK.

ISBN 978-1-84968-698-3

www.packtpub.com

Cover Image by Artie Ng (artherng@yahoo.com.au)

Credits

Author

Jose Luis Latorre Millas

Reviewers

Stephen Cleary

Layla Driscoll

Nauzad Kapadia

Leon Welicki

Ariel Woscoboinik

Acquisition Editor

Joanne Fitzpatrick

Lead Technical Editor

Dayan Hyames

Technical Editors

Chirag Jani

Soumya Kanti

Veena Pagare

Copy Editors

Insiya Morbiwala

Aditya Nair

Laxmi Subramanian

Project Coordinator

Amey Sawant

Proofreader

Lawrence A. Herman

Indexer

Rekha Nair

Production Coordinator

Manu Joseph

Cover Work

Manu Joseph

About the Author

Jose Luis Latorre Millas is a Microsoft Silverlight MVP, Toastmaster's Competent Communicator, TechEd speaker, INETA speaker, STEP member, trainer, technical writer, and reviewer. He is deeply involved with the technical communities through his collaboration with INETA Europe, Barcelona Developers, and other communities and user groups. He recently co-founded the Zurich .NET Developers user group at Zurich, Switzerland, which can be found at `http://ZurichDev.net`.

Jose Luis Latorre is strongly focused on XAML technologies such as Windows Store Apps, Windows Phone Apps, Silverlight, and WPF. He has written several articles on these topics, reviewed books, and worked with and given several talks over the last few years on these areas of knowledge.

Jose Luis works as UI Team Lead developer at Roche Diagnostics, where he does his best to develop and improve diagnostic software and its interfaces, which will help to save lives.

Acknowledgment

I'd like to first of all thank my girlfriend, Sandra Saenz Gonzalez, for her enormous support in taking on the project that this book was. I am greatly thankful for her constant understanding while having me closed up between four walls as I wrote and developed its contents. Thanks, Sandra, I love you.

Big thanks as well to my friend Jesus Salillas, who helped me with style reviews and guidance.

There are many good people out there who I have to thank, too. Thanks to Alfonso Rodriguez, who encouraged me to get into this "big .NET community world," and to Cristina Gonzalez, who has been my MVP Lead for—wow!—6 years already; easier said than done. Additionally, there is my good friend Paco Marin, who encouraged me strongly to write for him and his magazine, DotNetMania, now DNM, and during these years of collaboration, while writing for him, we have become good friends; thank you for all your support and care.

On the way, I found great friends out there, versed in the community, who allowed me to jump right at my passion. Thanks to the INETA guys, Damir Tomicic, Tomislav Bronzin, Sander Gerz, Andrej Radinjer, Andre Obelink, Christian Nagel, Dobrisa Adamec, and, of course, Miguel Lopez. Thank you for being there and doing what you do, greatly empowering the European developers' community. And for letting me take part in it and letting me "live it." One simple word—outstanding.

I'd like to give a big thank you to the staff of Packt Publishing for this opportunity, their support and patience on bringing this together, and for their understanding concerning my move to Switzerland, which had me a bit lost for a while (regarding the book). There you showcased that you are truly valuable, as a company and as people; special thanks to Rashmi Phadnis, Amey Sawant, and Dayan Hyames.

And finally I would like to thank Layla Driscoll, former Product Manager of the .NET CLR team, and Leon Welicki, Program Manager of the Workflow Foundation, both of whom I have had the honor of having as technical reviewers for this book. Thanks! It's awesome to count on you as reviewers.

I also have some friends who believed in me and encouraged me to write and said "I could do it"—thanks Braulio Diez, David Nudelman, Luis Franco, David Salgado, and Luis Fraile for your friendship, belief, and support.

I wouldn't have been able to write enclosed in the 15 square meters—my home for almost four months of my initial stay in Switzerland—if I couldn't take my stress out, which I did with my friends at Crossfit Zurich, so I want to give a big thank you to Ozi, all the coaches, and friends I have found at the "box" for being there!

And I will end by thanking those who started it all for me, that is, thanks to my father and mother for giving me birth and making me so curious; love you.

Thank you all!

About the Reviewers

Nauzad Kapadia is an independent professional and founder of Quartz Systems, and provides training and consulting services for the entire Microsoft .NET and SQL Server stack. Nauzad has over 17 years of industry experience and has been a regular speaker at events such as TechED, DevCon, DevDays, and user group events. He has been a Microsoft MVP (Most Valuable Professional) for six years on technologies ranging from C# and ASP.NET to SQL Server. Whenever he is not working on his computer, he enjoys rock music, photography, and reading.

Ariel Woscoboinik graduated as a Bachelor of Information Technology from the University of Buenos Aires, and as an IT technician from ORT school. Since his childhood he has been programing and getting more and more involved in the world of technology. Later on, he became interested in organizations and their business models and succeeded in converging both interests into his career—looking for the best solutions to involve people, processes, and technology.

Currently, he works as a Software Development Manager for Telefe, the leading TV channel in Argentina.

Ariel has been working with Microsoft technologies since high school. During his career, he has worked for highly prestigious companies from myriad industries—Microsoft, MAE, Intermex LLC, Pfizer, Monsanto, Banco Santander, IHSA, Disco S.A., Grupo Ecosistemas, Perception Group, and Conuar.

Among his passions are acting in dramas as an amateur actor, travelling around the world, watching films, and soccer.

You can reach him at http://www.linkedin.com/in/arielwoscoboinik or on twitter, @arielwos.

www.PacktPub.com

Support files, eBooks, discount offers and more

You might want to visit www.PacktPub.com for support files and downloads related to your book.

Did you know that Packt offers eBook versions of every book published, with PDF and ePub files available? You can upgrade to the eBook version at www.PacktPub.com and as a print book customer, you are entitled to a discount on the eBook copy. Get in touch with us at service@packtpub.com for more details.

At www.PacktPub.com, you can also read a collection of free technical articles, sign up for a range of free newsletters and receive exclusive discounts and offers on Packt books and eBooks.

http://PacktLib.PacktPub.com

Do you need instant solutions to your IT questions? PacktLib is Packt's online digital book library. Here, you can access, read and search across Packt's entire library of books.

Why Subscribe?

- ▶ Fully searchable across every book published by Packt
- ▶ Copy and paste, print and bookmark content
- ▶ On demand and accessible via web browser

Free Access for Packt account holders

If you have an account with Packt at www.PacktPub.com, you can use this to access PacktLib today and view nine entirely free books. Simply use your login credentials for immediate access.

Table of Contents

Preface   **1**

Chapter 1: Windows Store Apps   **7**

Introduction   7

Building our first Windows Store app   10

Adding a splash screen (and app tiles) to our app   21

Improving the application to make it compliant with the

Windows 8 lifecycle model   24

Improving our application tile   33

Improving our application with toast notifications   40

Chapter 2: Exploring the Top New Features of the CLR   **43**

Introduction   43

Creating a portable library   45

Controlling the timeout in regular expressions   49

Defining the culture for an application domain   52

Overriding the default reflection behavior   53

Using the new ZipArchive class   56

Understanding async and await in .NET 4.5   59

Using the new asynchronous file I/O operations   63

Chapter 3: Understanding the New Networking Capabilities   **67**

Introduction   67

Using the HttpClient and the new System.Net.Http namespaces   68

Chapter 4: Understanding the new features of Entity Framework 5.0   **75**

Introduction   75

Creating our first "Code First" application   76

Using Code First Migrations   84

Chapter 5: Understanding the New Features of ASP.NET   89

Introduction   89
Creating our first ASP.NET 4.5 Web Forms application   90
Configuring our application to use unobtrusive validation   103
Using Smart Tasks in the HTML editor   107
Using WAI-ARIA support   109
Using the Extract to User Control feature   110
Using the Page Inspector feature   112
Creating an asynchronous HTTP module   114

Chapter 6: Implementing WPF's new features   117

Introduction   117
Implementing asynchronous error handling with INotifyDataErrorInfo   118
Using the WeakEvent pattern with WeakEventManager   125
Using the dispatcher's new features   127
Data binding to static properties   130
Throttling data source update delays   133
LiveShaping – repositioning elements when its bound data changes   138

Chapter 7: Applying the New WCF Features   145

Introduction   145
Using the asynchronous features of WCF   145
Using WebSockets   149
Using Contract First development   156

Chapter 8: Creating and Hosting Our First ASP.NET Web API   161

Introduction   161
Creating our first ASP.NET web API   162
Implementing a CRUD ASP.NET web API   170
Setting up a self-hosted ASP.NET web API   175

Chapter 9: Using the New Capabilities of WF   181

Introduction   181
Creating a state machine workflow   182
Using the enhanced designer features   193

Appendix A: Resources for Further Knowledge   199

Resources for knowing more about .NET 4.5 and its tools   199
Resources for knowing more about Windows 8   200
Resources for knowing more about general development   201

Appendix B: .NET 4.5 – Deployment Risks and Issues   **203**

   Introduction   **203**

   Risks of the in-place upgrade   **204**

   Platform targeting   **204**

   Other risks   **205**

Index   **207**

Preface

With about 10 years since its first release, Microsoft's .NET Framework 4.5 is one of the most solid development technologies for creating casual, business, or enterprise applications. It has evolved into a very stable and solid framework for developing applications, with a solid core called the **CLR** (**Common Language Runtime**). Microsoft .NET Framework 4.5 includes massive changes and enables modern application and UI development.

Microsoft .NET Framework 4.5 Quickstart Cookbook aims to give you a runthrough of the most exciting features of the latest version. You will experience all the flavors of .NET 4.5 hands on. The "How-to" recipes mix the right ingredients for a final taste of the most appetizing features and characteristics. The book is written in a way that enables you to dip in and out of the chapters.

The book is full of practical code examples that are designed to clearly exemplify the different features and their applications in real-world development. All the chapters and recipes are progressive and based on the fresh features of .NET Framework 4.5.

The book is divided into functional examples that combine many techniques to showcase the usage of a concrete .NET 4.5 feature.

What this book covers

Chapter 1, Windows Store Apps, shows us the basics, 101, of creating Windows Store apps and some key aspects of it, such as adding a splash screen, tiles, understanding the Windows 8 lifecycle model, and using toasts.

Chapter 2, Exploring the Top New Features of the CLR, helps us explore some of the most exciting features of the CLR, such as portable class libraries, controlling timeout on regular expressions, overriding the default reflection behavior, and understanding how to use `async` and `await`.

Chapter 3, Understanding the New Networking Capabilities, explores the new networking features and show us how to use the `HttpClient` and `System.Net.Http` namespaces.

Chapter 4, Understanding the New Features of Entity Framework 5.0, helps us explore Code First and Code First Migrations directly.

Chapter 5, Understanding the New Features of ASP.NET, helps us explore the new capabilities while creating an ASP.NET web forms application; it shows us how to use unobtrusive validation and explains what it is good for; and it focuses on the other improvements, such as smart tasks, WAI-ARIA support, and "extract to user control" between others.

Chapter 6, Implementing WPF New Features, covers the new way of handling errors in WPF asynchronously with INotifyDataErrorInfo, use the WeakEvent pattern with the WeakEventManager class, bind to static properties, Throttling data source update delays and LiveShapping, and repositioning elements in the view when its bound data gets updated.

Chapter 7, Applying the New WCF's Features, helps us explore some of the most interesting features of WCF, such as its asynchronous support, WebSockets, and Contract First development.

Chapter 8, Creating and Hosting Our First ASP.NET Web API, basically explores this amazing new feature under the ASP.NET umbrella: web API. We will be creating a basic web API, adding CRUD capabilities, and self-hosting it.

Chapter 9, Using the New Capabilities of WF, explores one of the most exciting updates for .NET 4.5; it comes, greatly polished, with a mature and greatly enhanced framework for the workflow foundation. Here we explore creating a state machine workflow and new designer capabilities.

Appendix A, Resources for Further Knowledge, provides key references to websites of interest regarding the areas covered in this book.

Appendix B, NET 4.5, Deployment Risks and Issues, will show us some issues that can happen when applying .NET 4.5 to an existing project and on its deployment, such as the limitation on platform, different behaviors of the .NET framework, and that some things that might work properly in our developer environment might not work as well when deployed.

What you need for this book

For working through this book, .NET 4.5 is needed together with Visual Studio 2012; we recommend either the professional or a superior version. Regarding the operating system, Windows 8 is needed for some aspects as well, so it is the recommended operating system.

Who this book is for

If you are a .NET developer and would like to learn the new features in .NET 4.5, this book is just for you. Prior experience with .NET Framework would be useful but not necessary.

Microsoft .NET Framework 4.5 Quickstart Cookbook gives architects and project managers a high-level overview and clear understanding of what the .NET 4.5 Framework provides and how it can be used.

Conventions

In this book, you will find a number of styles of text that distinguish between different kinds of information. Here are some examples of these styles, and an explanation of their meaning.

Code words in text are shown as follows: "We can include other contexts through the use of the include directive."

A block of code is set as follows:

```
using System;
using System.Collections.Generic;
using System.Collections.ObjectModel;
using System.Linq;
using System.Text;
using System.Threading.Tasks;
```

When we wish to draw your attention to a particular part of a code block, the relevant lines or items are set in bold:

```
ToastTemplateType toastTemplate = ToastTemplateType.ToastText01;
XmlDocument toastXml = ToastNotificationManager.GetTemplateContent(to
astTemplate);
XmlNodeList toastTextElements = toastXml.GetElementsByTagName("text");
```

New terms and **important words** are shown in bold. Words that you see on the screen, in menus or dialog boxes for example, appear in the text like this: "clicking the **Next** button moves you to the next screen".

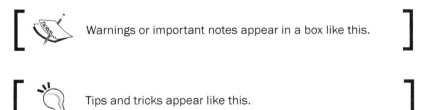

Warnings or important notes appear in a box like this.

Tips and tricks appear like this.

Reader feedback

Feedback from our readers is always welcome. Let us know what you think about this book—what you liked or may have disliked. Reader feedback is important for us to develop titles that you really get the most out of.

To send us general feedback, simply send an e-mail to feedback@packtpub.com, and mention the book title via the subject of your message.

If there is a topic that you have expertise in and you are interested in either writing or contributing to a book, see our author guide on www.packtpub.com/authors.

Customer support

Now that you are the proud owner of a Packt book, we have a number of things to help you to get the most from your purchase.

Downloading the example code

You can download the example code files for all Packt books you have purchased from your account at http://www.packtpub.com. If you purchased this book elsewhere, you can visit http://www.packtpub.com/support and register to have the files e-mailed directly to you.

Errata

Although we have taken every care to ensure the accuracy of our content, mistakes do happen. If you find a mistake in one of our books—maybe a mistake in the text or the code—we would be grateful if you would report this to us. By doing so, you can save other readers from frustration and help us improve subsequent versions of this book. If you find any errata, please report them by visiting http://www.packtpub.com/submit-errata, selecting your book, clicking on the **errata submission form** link, and entering the details of your errata. Once your errata are verified, your submission will be accepted and the errata will be uploaded on our website, or added to any list of existing errata, under the Errata section of that title. Any existing errata can be viewed by selecting your title from http://www.packtpub.com/support.

Piracy

Piracy of copyright material on the Internet is an ongoing problem across all media. At Packt, we take the protection of our copyright and licenses very seriously. If you come across any illegal copies of our works, in any form, on the Internet, please provide us with the location address or website name immediately so that we can pursue a remedy.

Please contact us at copyright@packtpub.com with a link to the suspected pirated material.

We appreciate your help in protecting our authors, and our ability to bring you valuable content.

Questions

You can contact us at questions@packtpub.com if you are having a problem with any aspect of the book, and we will do our best to address it.

1
Windows Store Apps

In this chapter, we will cover:

- ▶ Building our first Windows Store app
- ▶ Adding a splash screen (and app tiles) to our app
- ▶ Improving the application to make it compliant with the Windows 8 lifecycle model
- ▶ Improving our application tile
- ▶ Improving our application with toast notifications

Introduction

We are clearly speaking of a new, modern, and touch-friendly kind of application with the Windows Store apps style.

Windows Store app style application development, for the latest Windows 8 platform, is a very important part of this release of the .NET Framework 4.5.

We will explore Windows Runtime managed development in our development recipes. We also have the power of a very simple, well designed, and lightweight base class library API at our disposal (C# and VB) for developing Windows Store apps. This is called Windows Runtime, more commonly known as WinRT.

The following image clarifies the overall structure and components that we will have to use for developing Windows Store apps:

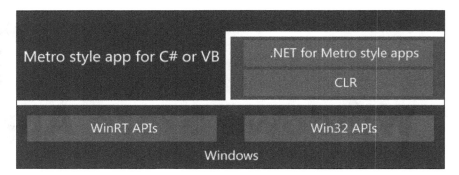

Portable libraries are there to help us port our existing code into multi-targeting scenarios such as Windows Store apps, Windows Phone, Silverlight, desktop, or X-box code with a strong focus on **Model-View-ViewModel** (**MVVM**). MVVM is an architectural design pattern designed for modern **user interface** (**UI**) development, very commonly used in XAML development. This will allow us to share the Model and ViewModel code with only the need for rewriting the UI and the application model, apart from the device integration.

Windows Store apps are designed for tablet devices and touch interaction, mainly for consumers. However, the good old desktop is still there and we can develop classic Windows applications, now called desktop apps, through the desktop mode.

Both of these execution and development modes coexist and are here for different scenarios. This chapter focuses on Windows Store apps development.

The Windows 8 app programming model basically:

- ▶ Implements the new Windows Store app style
- ▶ Provides a simple programming model for developers
- ▶ Provides WinRT, which provides a natural .NET-like interaction with Windows APIs
- ▶ Provides a Silverlight-like XAML UI model to develop with
- ▶ Is sandboxed, providing self-contained secure applications
- ▶ Is designed to be asynchronous, which if well applied, makes our applications fast and fluid

WinRT provides projections that expose the API to the different development environments. With this we can use WinRT from the .NET Framework 4.5.

The UI can be created with XAML (or HTML and CSS if we prefer), which is rendered with DirectX 11.1 (also known as Direct2D), so that we have a high performing UI. We can also implement the interface using DirectX.

So the good news is that the development is very straightforward and easy if we have some experience in Silverlight, **Windows Presentation Foundation** (**WPF**), or Windows Phone. If not, it will only be easy.

Note that the **Base Class Library** (**BCL**) used by WinRT is not the full desktop version but a reduced set, very similar to the Silverlight types.

There are also some very important Windows Store app principles to keep in mind. We will explore the following principles through the recipes in this book:

- **Windows Store app style design**: Focus on the content, minimalism, and emphasis on typography

- **Fast and fluid**: Fast user interactions and transitions that are intuitive and executed without delays (performance)

- **Touch first**: Simple and consistent touch interaction language

- **Scale beautifully**: Windows Store apps are readily executed on tablets with less than 10-inch and up to 27-inch screens

- **Support for multiple states**: Full screen, portrait, landscape, or snapped

- **Using the right contracts**: Contracts provide a way for Windows Store apps to collaborate, allowing the user to search or share content between applications

- **Live tiles**: Useful information appears on the app's tile on the start screen while the app is not in execution

- **Settings and data roam to the cloud**: Users get the same experience regardless of where they sign in from

It's your turn; go ahead and explore our recipes! They will help you explore progressively how to implement the different flavors of this new era of Windows Store apps. Let's get started!

Building our first Windows Store app

First things first; we will start with the creation of our first base application that we will re-use for most of the following recipes in this chapter, improving it one step (or more) at a time. This recipe will show you how to implement a basic application and help you get familiar with Visual Studio 2012 and Blend for Visual Studio 2012.

Getting ready

In order to use this recipe, you should have a Windows 8 operating system, Visual Studio 2012, and Blend for Visual Studio 2012. We will also need a Windows 8 developer license to create Windows Store apps, which we can get for free from Visual Studio 2012, as shown in the following image:

How to do it...

First we will open Visual Studio 2012 in Windows 8 and create a new project. For this we must perform the following steps:

1. Select the **Menu** option from **File | New Project** (or press *Ctrl + Shift + N*).

2. In the **New Project** window, we will select **Visual C#** from **Installed | Templates**. Then select the **Windows Store** app style and finally the **Grid App (XAML)** template. We will give it a proper name such as `OurFirstMetroApp`, and location, and click on the **OK** button.

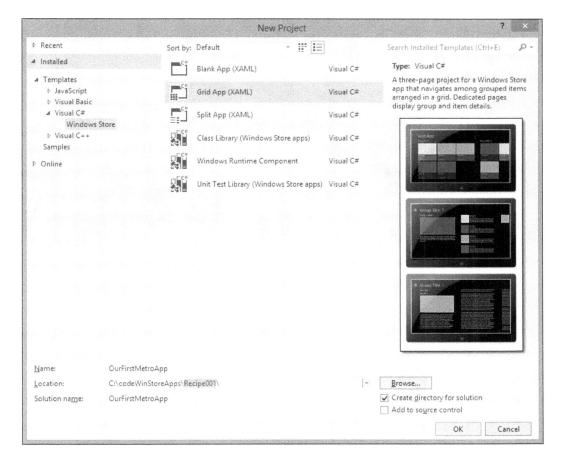

Next, Visual Studio will create the project for us.

3. We will build the solution from the menu option **Build | Build Solution** (or press *F7*) and then debug it from the menu option **Debug | Start Debugging** (we can also press *F5* or click on the play icon on the actions bar). If everything is working properly, we should get the following output:

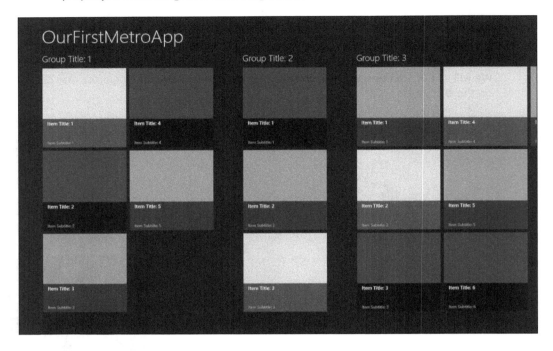

4. Now, we can scroll horizontally, click (or touch if we have a tactile screen) on a group title to open the group view, and click on an item title to open the item view. In the item view, we have buttons at the edges of the screen to navigate through the group items.

5. We will go back to the Windows 8 desktop mode, then to Visual Studio 2012 and stop the debugging session (or press *Shift + F5*).

6. Next, we will go to **Solution Explorer** and double-click on the `Package.appxmanifest` file.

7. Once the **Application Manifest Editor** window opens, we will go to the **Capabilities** tab and uncheck the **Internet (client) capability** option, as our current application does not need outbound access to the Internet.

8. To add a new item to the project, on the Visual Studio 2012 Solution Explorer right-click on the project and select **Add** | **New Item...** (or *Ctrl + Shift + A*).

9. Select the Windows Store app style, and from there select the **Basic Page** item, name it `HelloPage.xaml`, and then click on the **Add** button at the lower-right corner of the window.

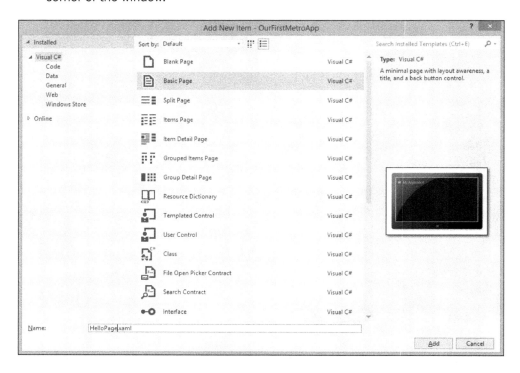

10. Open **HelloPage.xaml**, expand the design view, and then click on the **Unfold** button on the section that separates the WYSWIG render view of the XAML from the XAML code. There we will select **Fit all** at the left-hand side of the screen.

```
67%    ▼ ▦ ▦ ✛ ◄
800%      ↑↓      ⊡ XAML  ▣
400%    on:LayoutAwarePage
200%    :Name="pageRoot"
150%    :Class="OurFirstMetroApp.HelloPage"
        ataContext="{Binding DefaultViewModel, RelativeSource={RelativeSource Self}}"
100%    mlns="http://schemas.microsoft.com/winfx/2006/xaml/presentation"
66.67%  mlns:x="http://schemas.microsoft.com/winfx/2006/xaml"
50%     mlns:local="using:OurFirstMetroApp"
        mlns:common="using:OurFirstMetroApp.Common"
33.33%  mlns:d="http://schemas.microsoft.com/expression/blend/2008"
25%     mlns:mc="http://schemas.openxmlformats.org/markup-compatibility/2006"
12.5%   c:Ignorable="d">

Fit all      Page.Resources>
Fit selection
```

11. Let's add the finishing touches to our Visual Studio XAML workspace. To do so, we will expand the **TOOLBOX** and the **DOCUMENT OUTLINE** panels and pin them.

12. To use our project-defined name, we will comment the page's `AppName` resource, which is now overriding the global `AppName` resource. We will go and comment the line defining this on the `<Page.Resources>` tag of **HelloPage.xaml**, which is located in the topmost area of the XAML code, similar to the following code:

```
<Page.Resources>
<!-- TODO: Delete this line if the key AppName is declared in App.
xaml -->
<!--<x:String x:Key="AppName">My Application</x:String>-->
</Page.Resources>
```

13. Next, we will add a grid control to the bottom section of the design area by dragging it from the **TOOLBOX** panel and dropping it just below the title. It will be added inside the first grid and will appear on the **DOCUMENT OUTLINE** panel following the hierarchy.

14. We also want it to occupy all the available space on the grid row and column where we created it, so we will right-click on the grid, select **Reset Layout**, and then select **All**.

15. As the grid will handle the body section's layout, we will name it `grBody`. Select the grid and change the property **Name** on the **Properties** panel, or we can change it directly in the **DOCUMENT OUTLINE** panel.

16. Next, we will add a row separator to the `grBody` grid. We will move our cursor to the left-hand side of the grid, and an orange marker with the shape of an arrow will appear, indicating a grid separator. Clicking on that region, we will be able to add, modify, or delete a row. The same applies to the columns. We will add a row about 150 pixels from the bottom.

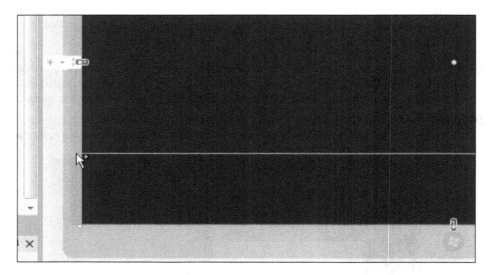

17. We will continue and change the size of the row to a fixed one. Select the row and move the cursor to the left-hand side of the blue zone that defines the row manipulation section. A pop-up menu will appear where we will choose the **Pixel** option for a fixed bottom row.

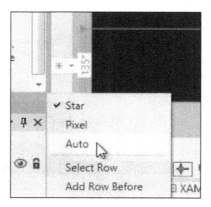

18. Next, we will add a **TextBlock** control on the top row of the grid that we just divided (adding a row separator creates two rows). We will reset the layout of the **TextBlock** control as we did previously with the grid.

19. Next, we will style the **TextBlock** using a default style by right-clicking on the **TextBlock** and then selecting the option **Edit Style | Apply Resource | PageSubheaderTextStyle**.

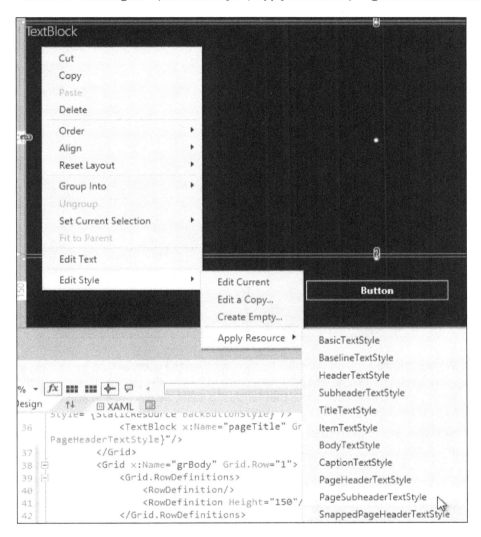

20. To finish the **TextBlock**, we will edit the **Text** property in the **Properties** panel by writing This is our First Windows Store App.

21. We will drag a **Button** control from **TOOLBOX** to the lower row of the grid that we added recently. We will change some of its properties in the **Properties** panel, setting its **HorizontalAlignment** and **VerticalAlignment** to **Center**, its **FontSize** to **20**, its **Name** to btnStart, and its **Content** to Start.

22. Next, we will change its font style property. For this we will click on the box next to the property and select **System Resource** and then **ContentControlThemeFontFamily**.

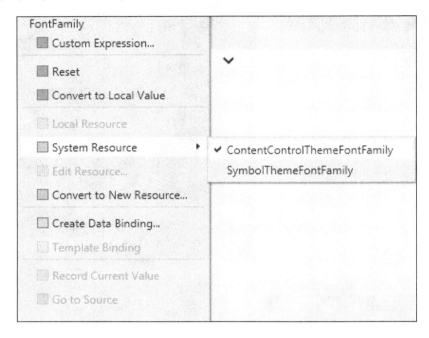

23. We will double-click on the start button and then the code behind HelloPage .xaml will be seen, where an empty method has been created. There we will enter the following code (note that for this to work, we will have to add the data to the namespace):

```
private void btnStart_Click(object sender, RoutedEventArgs e)
{
this.Frame.Navigate(typeof(GroupedItemsPage), "AllGroups");
}
```

24. We will open the App.xaml.cs code behind the file and comment the Navigate instruction on the OnLaunched event, adding a new one that brings us to HelloPage.xaml:

```
//if (!rootFrame.Navigate(typeof(GroupedItemsPage), "AllGroups"))
if (!rootFrame.Navigate(typeof(HelloPage)))
```

25. Next, we will save all from the menu or with the *Ctrl + Shift + S* shortcut.

26. We will build the solution and debug our first Windows Store app. We should see that our application launches and shows the page we just added.

How it works...

We created an application from the **Grid Application** template, which does a lot of work for us, creating an app that allows us to navigate through a hierarchy of groups and group items. We can explore them in the touch-ready Windows Store app `GridView` (the Windows Store app control that displays a grid of data items) and from there we can go to the group view and the item view, where we can navigate to other items.

If we look at the structure that has been created for us by the project template, we have the typical **Properties** and **References** sections of a Visual Studio .NET project. The `App.xaml` file is the entry point to our application and has the same meaning and overall structure as the same file on Silverlight, WPF, or Windows Phone projects containing defined or referenced global resources. When the application starts, it creates a frame-based navigation system, similar to that of the Windows Phone, and navigates to our first page, in our case, **HelloPage.xaml**.

To move between pages, the code behind `App.xaml` creates a frame and adds it as the application's main content. The navigation actions just change the page contained by the frame, and the navigation stack is maintained for us so we can go forward and navigate back automatically. The following diagram explains it clearly:

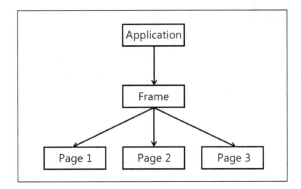

So, we can navigate to a particular page with the following instruction:

```
this.Frame.Navigate(typeof(GroupedItemsPage), "AllGroups");
```

The previous instruction indicates the page we want to navigate to and the navigation parameter. Additionally we can navigate back with the following instruction:

```
if (this.Frame.CanGoBack) {
this.Frame.GoBack();
}
```

Note that the `CanGoback` check is not obligatory, but not doing so can throw an exception.

We have also specified the application's capabilities through the `Package.appxmanifest` designer.

We added a basic page of type `LayoutAwarePage`, which provides layout awareness, that is, this page is now able to detect changes in how it is viewed. This can be either portrait, landscape, snapped, or filled. Being the two last ones (snapped and filled) special views of the application provided by the Windows Store App design style that our application is expected to support.

On our basic page, we deleted a resource so the page could get the `app.xaml` file predefined. The `AppName` resource added a grid with some layout and two controls to it, **TextBlock** and **Button**. Then we adjusted their layout and properties to change the default application behavior with the click event of the start button. We finally changed the default code of the `App.xaml.cs` `OnLaunched` method to navigate to our new page instead of the previous `GroupedItemsPage` location.

Moreover, we have been doing several tasks in various ways with Visual Studio 2012 so now we should be more familiar with it.

There's more...

Other options to create our Windows Store app would be to create a blank application or a split application. The blank application creates an extremely basic application structure for us to fill. The split application shows information in a master-detail way, showing the master information on one half of the screen and the details on the other half.

There are also the classic **Class Library** and **Unit Test Library** templates.

We have built this first project as a grid application as we will use it for further recipes, adding more features to it so that it becomes a fully compliant Windows Store app style application.

With this recipe, we have also created an application and extended it with a first page and made it compliant with the Windows Store app style design and principles, providing a clean and open layout that minimizes distractions, with enough breathing room and a clear information hierarchy founded on a clean typography.

Adding a splash screen (and app tiles) to our app

So, we have an application and want to take full advantage of the Windows Store app style design, right? One of the easiest ways of accomplishing this is to provide a splash screen.

Getting ready

We should have an application ready, such as the previous recipe app. Any app will do. In fact, you can create an empty project and you will be ready to start this recipe.

How to do it...

Here we are going to take some steps to provide our app with a splash screen and app. tiles. There are some predefined places in our app that we can customize with default images.

1. We will put an image in our splash screen that consists of a background color and an image of 620 x 300 pixels. We already have a default image, SplashScreen.png, in the Assets folder so we will need to replace this image with our own.

2. We will also prepare our application logo in three flavors, 150 x 150 pixels for our main logo, 50 x 50 pixels for our store logo, and 30 x 30 pixels for our small logo image.

3. Additionally, we can add a `Wide Logo` image to display when the application goes on expanded mode, in which case our tile doubles its space. Thus, we must make a tile of 310 x 150 pixels.

4. Next, we will add the images to our `Assets` folder, replacing the current predefined placeholder images with the new ones for our project.

5. Following that, we will open the `Package.appxmanifest` file with the manifest designer; a double-click on the file will do. Add a reference at the **Wide logo** section of our new wide logo. Then we will change the **Show name** section to **No Logos**, as our logo will showcase the application name. And finally we will change **Background color** to #FFFFFF.

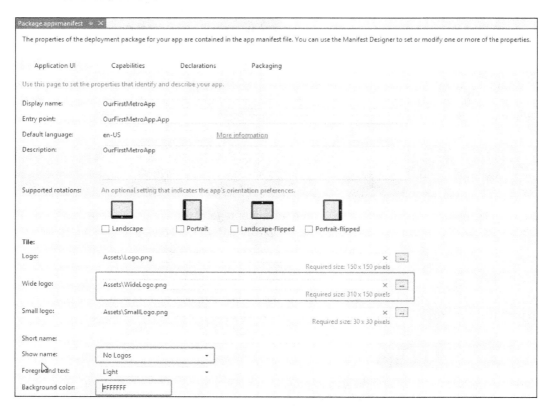

6. We will deploy our solution to see how it fits in the Windows 8 UI. We should locate quickly our application tile, select it and make it larger, and launch it to see our brand new custom splash screen.

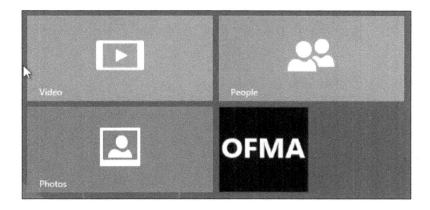

The custom splash screen after launching will look something like this:

How it works...

We just added some graphical assets and changed completely how the application looks in the Windows 8 UI, re-styling it and providing it with a bit of branding. Our app is now much closer to the Windows Store app design style.

We have also shown how easy this is and explained some of the properties from the `Package.appxmanifest` file.

There's more...

We could use additional splash screens for 1.4x and 1.8x scaling if we want better adaptation for higher resolution displays.

We could also capture the `SplashScreen.Dismissed` event and react quickly to it, for example, to provide a follow-up screen that mimics the splash screen while our application loads.

This behavior would be beneficial if the application has to perform some processing or data loading/caching before providing control to the user.

The official **Microsoft Developer Network** (**MSDN**) splash screen sample, for example, exhibits this precise behavior.

Another option would be to start the transition to our application's main screen after the `SplashScreen.Dismissed` event.

Improving the application to make it compliant with the Windows 8 lifecycle model

An important requirement for a Windows Store app is that it should comply with the Windows 8 UI lifecycle model, which is to save its state and important data when we stop using the application. So if it gets unloaded from memory, we can restore its state without any problem. It gives our application a good **user experience** (**UX**) and aligns itself with the expectations of the customers, in that when we open it back, it will seem as if it has never been closed.

Getting ready

As any Windows Store app would do, we propose evolving the resultant application from the previous recipe.

How to do it...

Here we will add some data to showcase the lifecycle steps that our application goes through, binding it to our interface and feeding it while stepping through the lifecycle events. To do this, we should start from the app resulting from our previous recipe.

1. In the `DataModel` folder, we will add a new class named `AppData.cs`.

2. Next we will add the following code to it:

```
using System;
using System.Collections.Generic;
using System.Collections.ObjectModel;
using System.Linq;
using System.Text;
using System.Threading.Tasks;

namespace OurFirstMetroApp.DataModel
{
public class AppData : OurFirstMetroApp.Common.BindableBase
    {
private string _appKeyValue = string.Empty;
public string AppKeyValue
        {
get { return this._appKeyValue; }
set { this.SetProperty(ref this._appKeyValue, value); }
        }
    }
}
```

3. We will open `App.xaml.cs`, and, in the `constructor` method, locate the following line of code:

```
this.Suspending += OnSuspending;
```

4. Add the following lines of code to implement the event handler of the `Resuming` event as the `Suspending` event is already handled. There we will accept the automatically created method that Visual Studio proposes after pressing += and the *Tab* key. The code should end as follows:

```
//We handle the suspending event to save the state
this.Suspending += OnSuspending;
//And the Resuming to control when we resume our app.
this.Resuming += App_Resuming;
```

5. After this, we will add the `MyAppBindableData` property in the `App` class at `App.cs`:

```
Public AppData MyAppBindableData{ get; set; }
```

6. We might need to add a reference to the `DataModel` namespace:

```
using OurFirstMetroApp.DataModel;
```

7. We will initialize the `MyAppBindableData` property in the application's constructor with the following code:

```
//We initialize the AppBindableData
this.MyAppBindableData = new AppData();
```

8. Next we will add the following code onto the `Suspending` event handler method:

```
private async void OnSuspending(object sender, SuspendingEventArgs e)
{
SaveUserSessionData();
}
```

9. Note that there is already an implementation doing some work. We will avoid exploring or re-using that code for simplicity, but it would be a good exercise to explore the code, which is in the `SuspensionManager.cs` source file in the `Common` folder of the project.

10. Add the `SaveUserSessionData` method as follows at the end of the `App` class:

```
private void SaveUserSessionData()
{
    //Save application state and stop any background activity
ApplicationDataContainer localSettings = null;
localSettings = ApplicationData.Current.LocalSettings;
localSettings.Values["KeyValue"] = " - I have been suspended ";
}
```

11. Note that we will have to add a reference to the `Windows.Storage` namespace:

```
using Windows.Storage;
```

12. Implementing the other generated function, `App_Resuming`, will result in the following code:

```
Void App_Resuming(object sender, object e)
{
PrepareMessage (" and resumed");
}
```

13. To implement the `PrepareMessage` method, we will code it as follows:

```
Void PrepareMessage(String msg) {
ApplicationDataContainer localSettings = null;
localSettings = ApplicationData.Current.LocalSettings;
var kv = localSettings.Values["KeyValue"];
```

```
if (kv != null)
    {
this.MyAppBindableData.AppKeyValue = this.MyAppBindableData.
AppKeyValue + kv.ToString();
    }
this.MyAppBindableData.AppKeyValue = this.MyAppBindableData.
AppKeyValue + msg;
}
```

14. Next we will override the application's `OnActivated` event by adding the following code:

```
protected override void OnActivated(IActivatedEventArgs args)
{
    String msg = String.Empty;
if (args.Kind == ActivationKind.Launch) {
msg = msg + " - Previously I was " + args.PreviousExecutionState.
ToString();
msg = msg + " and have been Activated";
    }
PrepareMessage(msg);
base.OnActivated(args);
}
```

15. Next we will manage the application's `OnLaunched` method by adding the following code at the end of the method:

```
String msg = String.Empty;
if (args.Kind == ActivationKind.Launch)
{
msg = msg + " - Previously I was " + args.PreviousExecutionState.
ToString();
msg = msg + " and have been Launched";
}
PrepareMessage(msg);
```

16. To wire this all up, we will go to our `HelloPage.xaml` page, and there we will create `TextBlock` that we will name as `tbAppLifeHistory`, binding this text property to the `AppKeyValue` property. We will locate it under the first `TextBlock` code of the application description. Note that we will have to add a row to the grid to properly position this new control. The result can be seen as follows:

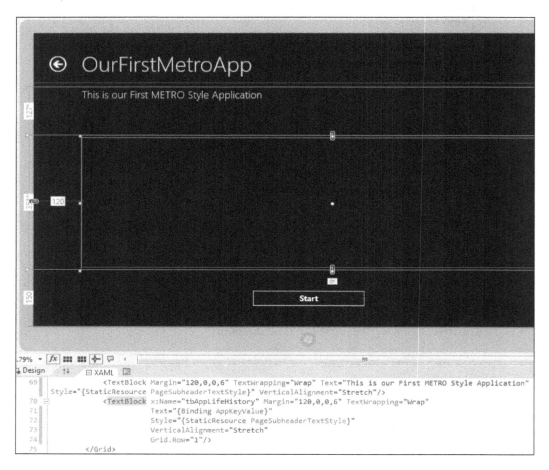

17. The XAML code for the `TextBlock` will look as follows:

```
<TextBlock x:Name="tbAppLifeHistory" Margin="120,0,0,6"
TextWrapping="Wrap"
Text="{Binding AppKeyValue}"
Style="{StaticResource PageSubheaderTextStyle}"
VerticalAlignment="Stretch"
Grid.Row="1"/>
```

18. To finish our wiring, we will go to the code behind `HelloPage.xaml` and on the constructor, add a call to the `CheckPreviousExecution()` method as follows:

```
Void CheckPreviousExecution() {
this.tbAppLifeHistory.DataContext = (App.Current as App).
MyAppBindableData;

ApplicationDataContainer localSettings = null;
localSettings = ApplicationData.Current.LocalSettings;
localSettings.Values["KeyValue"]="";
}
```

19. Note that we will have to add a `usings` clause for the `Windows.Storage` namespace.

20. Now we just have to compile and try it. A good way is to build and then deploy the solution to our Windows 8 operating system. We can use the menu option **Build | Deploy Solution**. We could also use the simulator and suspend/resume it.

21. Next we will go to our Windows 8 UI and run it. The first time we run our application, we will see the following message:

22. Now we will go to desktop mode where we will launch the **Task Manager** window. After approximately 5 seconds, we will see that our application goes into the **Suspended** state. Note that an easy way to launch the **Task Manager** is to right-click on the bottom taskbar and then click on **Task Manager**.

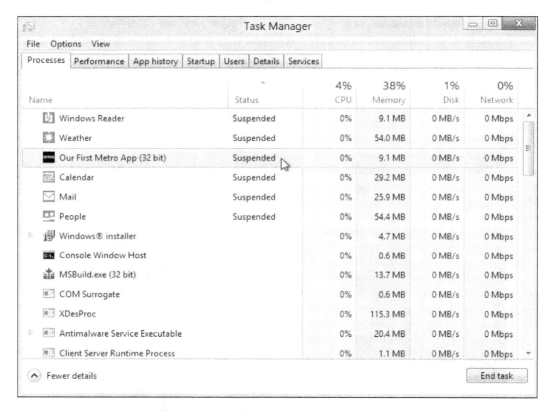

23. Go back to the Windows 8 UI and launch our application again. This is what we will see:

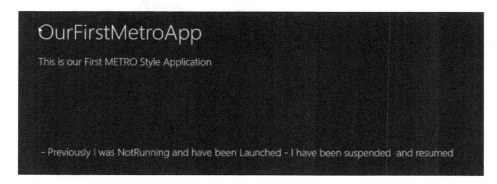

24. Next we will go back to the desktop mode and terminate the application from the **Task Manager**. If we go back to the Windows 8 UI and launch our application, this is what we will see:

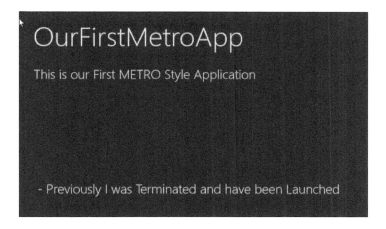

How it works...

We started creating the AppData class that inherits from BindableBase, which in turn implements the INotifyPropertyChanged interface and is used to notify the value changes in a property that we have bound to the user interface through binding.

Next we add an AppData property in our application class so that we can reference this property globally anywhere within our application.

Continuing, we will handle the suspending and resuming events that occur when the application is suspended, which will happen after we switch to another task or application. After 5 seconds, our application will save its state and become **Suspended**. In our case, we will only indicate that our application has been suspended.

For that we have the SaveUserSessionData() method responsible. There we will access our application data through the application data's ApplicationDataContainer class where we can store the settings and other information belonging to our application. The ApplicationDataContainer class is a private storage for our application and current user that we can access in many different ways, such as the key-to-value dictionary or through a filesystem-like method. This is very similar to Silverlight's isolated storage and if you have used it before it should feel very familiar.

For the resuming event, we are calling the PrepareMessage method. We will pass one message string to it and it will fetch the value from our application's localSettings property and concatenate it with the message, adding it to the AppKeyValue property.

Basically we are indicating our application lifecycle status changes and are concatenating them on a global property.

To finish, we must indicate the changes on the `OnActivated` and `OnLaunched` methods; there we will also add the `PreviousExecutionState` enumeration to the message that declares the original state from which the application comes.

We then added `TextBlock` control and bound it to the `AppKeyValue` property. In the code, we added its data context to the corresponding property of the application class holding this property; we did this to separate it from the `App.cs` class implementation and to take advantage of the `BindableBase` base class that the template had already provided.

We have also seen how to deploy our application, launch the task manager, and control our application states from it.

To properly understand the states, we have the following diagram:

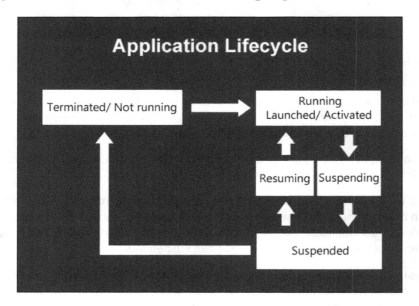

Here we see clearly that when the application is not running, it can be put into the terminated (on purpose) or the not running (nobody terminated it, we just installed or deployed it, for example) state.

Then, we can launch it from the Windows 8 UI and the application will be in the running state. From this state we can close or terminate it or we can move to another application or window. After 5 seconds, our application will be automatically suspended. If we come back to it, our application will resume and get activated (not launched, as this would happen when we do it from the terminated or the not running state).

The application will remain as it was when it was suspended and we will have no clue that it has stopped its execution, unless we code the application to be aware of it.

There's more...

It could be a good idea to save the user state and the application data, for example, if the user was working on a form. It would be nice that when he returns, he goes back to the same form he was working on and finds the same data.

If the application has been deactivated for a long period of time, a recommended practice would be to start afresh, as the user might not remember what was happening or where he was. Of course, it all depends on the application and the tasks being performed in it.

If the application works with online data, the activated and resuming events could be used to refresh the information from the online sources. For example, we could have an app with a financial purpose or our app is alive such as a chat, RSS reader, or a twitter app.

We could also associate our app with a file or a protocol so that it would be the default application for managing these file extensions or we could define auto-launching capabilities for AutoPlay or other contracts and extensions. Some possible contracts might be the camera, contact picker, print task, protocol, search, or share target.

Improving our application tile

One of the principles of the Windows Store style apps is to invest in a great tile. As the entry point to our applications and the main point of interaction with the Windows 8 UI, it is obviously extremely important.

A tile is the main interface of our application in the Windows 8 UI, which can provide a much more engaging experience than a traditional icon, as it is much more personal. We can update it while our app is not running, thereby keeping it alive.

We will dedicate this recipe to improving our application's main tile.

Getting ready

We will implement this recipe on the application we have been developing, but we could apply what we are going to do to any Windows Store app.

How to do it...

Here we are going to see how to add notification capabilities to our application tile.

1. Open the application and, from the project, open `App.xaml.cs` and add the following namespaces:

```
using Windows.UI.Notifications;
using Windows.Data.Xml.Dom;
```

2. Create a method with the name `CreateTileNotification` using the following code:

```
private void CreateTileNotification() {
    //Wide Tile
XmlDocument tileXml = TileUpdateManager.GetTemplateContent(TileTem
plateType.TileWideText03);
XmlNodeList tileTextAttributes = tileXml.
GetElementsByTagName("text");
tileTextAttributes[0].AppendChild(tileXml.CreateTextNode("A group
was added or updated..."));

    //Square Tile
XmlDocument squareTileXml = TileUpdateManager.GetTemplateContent(T
ileTemplateType.TileSquareText04);
XmlNodeList SquareTileTextAttributes = squareTileXml.
GetElementsByTagName("text");
SquareTileTextAttributes[0].AppendChild(squareTileXml.
CreateTextNode("A group was added or updated..."));

    //We add the square tile to the wide tile as a sibling of the
wide tile
IXmlNode node = tileXml.ImportNode(squareTileXml.
GetElementsByTagName("binding").Item(0), true);
tileXml.GetElementsByTagName("visual").Item(0).AppendChild(node);

    //We create the notification with the tiles and send it to the
app tile
TileNotification tileNotification = new TileNotification(tileXml);
tileNotification.ExpirationTime = DateTimeOffset.UtcNow.
AddSeconds(10);
TileUpdateManager.CreateTileUpdaterForApplication().
Update(tileNotification);
}
```

3. Add a call to this method at the end of the `OnLaunched` method:

```
CreateTileNotification();
```

4. We will open `Package.appxmanifest` and under the **Tile:** section, put #222222 as the **Background color** property.

5. We should execute the application and immediately go back to the Windows 8 UI to see the tile update in action.

6. In the `OnLaunched` method, just before the `CreateTileNotification();` call, we will add the following lines of code to enable notification cycling:

```
//We enable the notification cycling
TileUpdateManager.CreateTileUpdaterForApplication().
EnableNotificationQueue(true);
```

7. Next we are going to update our `CreateTileNotification` method to accept two string parameters, one for the message and another for the tag of the notification, which will serve to uniquely identify a notification in our app. Add the following code:

```
private void CreateTileNotification(String msg, String Tag)
{
    //Wide Tile
XmlDocument tileXml = TileUpdateManager.GetTemplateContent(TileTem
plateType.TileWideText03);
XmlNodeList tileTextAttributes = tileXml.
GetElementsByTagName("text");
tileTextAttributes[0].AppendChild(tileXml.CreateTextNode(msg));

    //Square Tile
XmlDocument squareTileXml = TileUpdateManager.GetTemplateContent(T
ileTemplateType.TileSquareText04);
XmlNodeList SquareTileTextAttributes = squareTileXml.
GetElementsByTagName("text");
SquareTileTextAttributes[0].AppendChild(squareTileXml.
CreateTextNode(msg));
```

```
        //We add the square tile to the wide tile as a sibling of the
wide tile
IXmlNode node = tileXml.ImportNode(squareTileXml.
GetElementsByTagName("binding").Item(0), true);
tileXml.GetElementsByTagName("visual").Item(0).AppendChild(node);

        //We create the notification with the tiles and send it to the
app tile
TileNotification tileNotification = new TileNotification(tileXml);

        //We add a tag to the tileNotification
tileNotification.Tag = Tag;

tileNotification.ExpirationTime = DateTimeOffset.UtcNow.
AddSeconds(10);
TileUpdateManager.CreateTileUpdaterForApplication().
Update(tileNotification);
        }
```

8. We will substitute the previous `CreateTileNotification()` call that we added at the end of the `OnLaunched` event handler with these new lines:

```
CreateTileNotification("Message number one", "one");
CreateTileNotification("Message number two", "two");
CreateTileNotification("Message number three", "three");
```

9. Launch the application and immediately after launching it go back to our Windows 8 UI. Watch how the tile now shows the three message tiles in a cycle that repeats itself.

10. After the latest `CreateTileNotification` call, add the following code:

```
//We add a Numeric badge
XmlDocument badgeXml = BadgeUpdateManager.GetTemplateContent(Badge
TemplateType.BadgeNumber);
XmlElement badgeElement = (XmlElement)badgeXml.SelectSingleNode("/
badge");
```

```
badgeElement.SetAttribute("value", "7");
BadgeNotification badge = new BadgeNotification(badgeXml);
BadgeUpdateManager.CreateBadgeUpdaterForApplication().
Update(badge);
```

11. If we now run the application, we will observe a number at the bottom-right corner; that's our numeric badge.

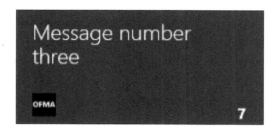

12. We will comment the previous code and add these lines after it:

```
//And we add a Glyph badge
XmlDocument badgeXml_Glyph = BadgeUpdateManager.GetTemplateContent
(BadgeTemplateType.BadgeGlyph);
XmlElement badgeElement_Glyph = (XmlElement)badgeXml_Glyph.
SelectSingleNode("/badge");
badgeElement_Glyph.SetAttribute("value", "newMessage");
BadgeNotification badge_Glyph = new BadgeNotification(badgeXml_
Glyph);
BadgeUpdateManager.CreateBadgeUpdaterForApplication().
Update(badge_Glyph);
```

13. Run the application and switch immediately to see the new look of our application tile with a glyph badge.

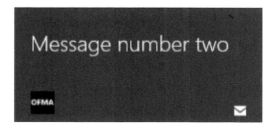

How it works...

First, we picked a template for our tile and loaded it into an `XmlDocument` variable.

```
XmlDocument tileXml = TileUpdateManager.GetTemplateContent(TileTemplat
eType.TileWideText03);
```

Next we accessed the element that we wanted to change from within the template and changed its value.

```
XmlNodeList tileTextAttributes = tileXml.GetElementsByTagName("text");
tileTextAttributes[0].AppendChild(tileXml.CreateTextNode("A group was
added or updated..."));
```

We repeated the same operation but with another `SquareTile` template, so we ended up with two customized tile templates.

```
//Square Tile
XmlDocument squareTileXml = TileUpdateManager.GetTemplateContent(TileT
emplateType.TileSquareText04);
XmlNodeList SquareTileTextAttributes = squareTileXml.
GetElementsByTagName("text");
SquareTileTextAttributes[0].AppendChild(squareTileXml.
CreateTextNode("A group was added or updated..."));
```

Then we added the square tile as a sibling of the wide tile.

```
//We add the square tile to the wide tile as a sibling of the wide
tile
IXmlNode node = tileXml.ImportNode(squareTileXml.
GetElementsByTagName("binding").Item(0), true);
tileXml.GetElementsByTagName("visual").Item(0).AppendChild(node);
```

Once the tile XML code was ready, we created `TileNotification` from it.

```
//We create the notification with the tiles and send it to the app
tile
TileNotification tileNotification = new TileNotification(tileXml);
```

Then we added an expiration time for the tile to go away after 10 seconds.

```
tileNotification.ExpirationTime = DateTimeOffset.UtcNow.AddSeconds(10);
```

We ended by sending `createdTilenotification` to `TileUpdater` of our application.

```
TileUpdateManager.CreateTileUpdaterForApplication().
Update(tileNotification);
```

We enabled the cycling tile notifications, which allow us to show various notifications one after another in a queue with instructions:

```
TileUpdateManager.CreateTileUpdaterForApplication().
EnableNotificationQueue(true);
```

And then we created `TileNotification` with a tag to differentiate between different `TileNotifications` while removing `ExpirationTime`.

Continuing our recipe, we created in a similar way the numeric badge from a template (basic badge templates are `BadgeNumber` or `BadgeGlyph`) and then set the badge attribute, created the `BadgeNotification`, and used `BadgeUpdateManager` to update it.

A `BadgeNumber` template can display a number from 1 to 99 and a `BadgeGlyph` template can contain one of the following status glyphs:

- `none`
- `activity`
- `alert`
- `available`
- `away`
- `busy`
- `newMessage`
- `paused`
- `playing`
- `unavailable`
- `error`

We have seen that improving a tile with custom notifications or cycling through different tile notifications are easy to implement. Moreover, we have a good number of tile templates to explore.

Creating badges is also really easy and might add a lot of value to our application tile.

We should use tile improvements, notifications, and badges with care and only when they make sense and add value to our application.

We could also implement secondary tiles in response to user actions.

Finally, we can update the tile while the application is not running through the **Windows Push Notification Service** (**WNS**), improving our app with toast notifications.

Improving our application with toast notifications

Toasts notify the user of relevant and time-sensitive events such as the reception of a new e-mail or a reminder for an approaching appointment.

They will help our application to accomplish another of the Windows Store app principles, which is to feel connected and alive.

Getting ready

We will implement this recipe on the application that we have been developing, but we could apply what we are going to do to any Windows Store app.

How to do it...

Here we are going to add the capability of creating toasts to our app.

1. Open the application and `HelloPage.xaml.cs` and add the following `using` namespaces:

   ```
   using Windows.Data.Xml.Dom;
   using Windows.UI.Notifications;
   ```

   Add there the following method:
   ```
   private void GenerateToastNotification()
   {
   ToastTemplateType toastTemplate = ToastTemplateType.ToastText01;
   XmlDocument toastXml = ToastNotificationManager.GetTemplateContent
   (toastTemplate);
   XmlNodeList toastTextElements = toastXml.
   GetElementsByTagName("text");
   ```

```
toastTextElements[0].AppendChild(toastXml.CreateTextNode("A
toast!"));
    //The duration
XmlNodeList rootElement = toastXml.GetElementsByTagName("toast");
    ((XmlElement)rootElement[0]).SetAttribute("duration", "long");
    //Create and send the toast
ToastNotification toast = new ToastNotification(toastXml);
ToastNotificationManager.CreateToastNotifier().Show(toast);
}
```

2. Open `HelloPage.xaml`. Add a button near the header with the text `Generate Toast`.

3. On the code behind the click event handler of the added button, add a call to the newly created `GenerateToastNotification()` method.

4. Open the `Package.appmanifest` designer and on the **Application UI** tab, we will look for the **Toast Capable** option and select **Yes** on the combobox.

5. If we execute the application and click a number of times on the **Launch Toast** button, our display should look similar to the following image:

How it works...

In a way very similar to our tile notification, we picked up the toast template type and loaded the template content into an `XmlDocument` variable.

After this we accessed the element that we wanted to change, in our case the `text` element, and changed its value.

We changed its duration by setting one of the attributes of the toast element.

Finally, we created `ToastNotification` from the resulting XML and showed the toast.

There's more...

We could navigate to a specific destination in our app when the user taps on the toast, as that might be an invitation to explore new and interesting data.

We can use different toast templates, schedule toast notifications, or even send toast push notifications through the WNS.

The toast can be extensively customized with images, sounds, or an expiration time.

2
Exploring the Top New Features of the CLR

In this chapter, we will cover:

- ► Creating a portable library
- ► Controlling the timeout in regular expressions
- ► Defining the culture for an application domain
- ► Overriding the default reflection behavior
- ► Using the new ZipArchive class
- ► Understanding async and await in .NET 4.5
- ► Using the new asynchronous file I/O operations

Introduction

.NET 4.5 brings many benefits, such as improvements in performance, compatibility, garbage collection, and new features in its structure to provide the overall scenarios it is targeted for, for example, Windows Store apps development.

One of its most important characteristics is that it is an in-place substitution of the .NET 4.0 and only runs on Windows Vista SP2 or later systems.

.NET 4.5 breathes asynchronous features and makes writing async code even easier. It also provides us with the **Task Parallel Library** (**TPL**) Dataflow Library to help us create parallel and concurrent applications.

Another very important addition is the portable libraries, which allow us to create managed assemblies that we can refer through different target applications and platforms, such as Windows 8, Windows Phone, Silverlight, and Xbox.

We couldn't avoid mentioning **Managed Extensibility Framework** (**MEF**), which now has support for generic types, a convention-based programming model, and multiple scopes.

Of course, this all comes together with a brand-new tooling, Visual Studio 2012, which you can find at `http://msdn.microsoft.com/en-us/vstudio`. Just be careful if you have projects in .NET 4.0 since it is an in-place install.

> For this chapter I'd like to give a special thanks to Layla Driscoll from the Microsoft .NET team who helped me summarize the topics, focus on what's essential, and showcase it to you, dear reader, in the most efficient way possible. Thanks, Layla.

There are some features that we will not be able to explore through recipes as they are just there and are part of the CLR but are worth explaining for better understanding:

- Support for arrays larger than 2 GB on 64-bit platforms, which can be enabled by an option in the app config file.
- Improved performance on the server's background garbage collection, which must be enabled in the `<gcServer>` element in the runtime configuration schema.
- **Multicore JIT**: Background JIT (Just In Time) compilation on multicore CPUs to improve app performance. This basically creates profiles and compiles methods that are likely to be executed on a separate thread.
- Improved performance for retrieving resources.
- The culture-sensitive string comparison (sorting, casing, normalization, and so on) is delegated to the operating system when running on Windows 8, which implements Unicode 6.0. On other platforms, the .NET framework will behave as in the previous versions, including its own string comparison data implementing Unicode 5.0.

Next we will explore, in practice, some of these features to get a solid grasp on what .NET 4.5 has to offer and, believe me, we will have our hands full!

Creating a portable library

Most of us have often struggled and hacked our code to implement an assembly that we could use in different .NET target platforms. Portable libraries are here to help us to do exactly this.

Now there is an easy way to develop a portable assembly that works without modification in .NET Framework, Windows Store apps style, Silverlight, Windows Phone, and XBOX 360 applications.

The trick is that the Portable Class Library project supports a subset of assemblies from these platforms, providing us a Visual Studio template.

This recipe will show you how to implement a basic application and help you get familiar with Visual Studio 2012.

Getting ready

In order to use this recipe you should have Visual Studio 2012 installed. Note that you will need a Visual Studio 2012 SKU higher than Visual Studio Express for it to fully support portable library projects.

How to do it...

Here we will create a portable library and see how it works:

1. First, open Visual Studio 2012 and create a new project. We will select the **Portable Class Library** template from the **Visual C#** category.

2. Now open the **Properties** dialog box of our newly created portable application and, in the library we will see a new section named **Target frameworks**. Note that, for this type of project, the dialog box will open as soon as the project is created, so opening it will only be necessary when modifying it afterwards.

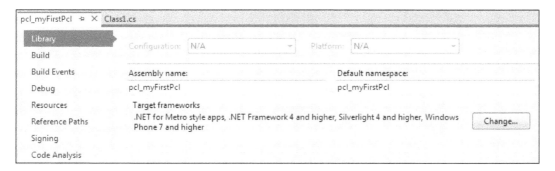

3. If we click on the **Change** button, we will see all the multitargeting possibilities for our class.

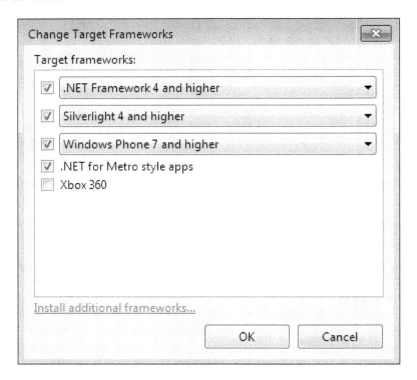

4. We will see that we can target different versions of a framework. There is also a link to install additional frameworks. The one that we could install right now is XNA but we will click on **Cancel** and let the dialog box be as it is.

5. Next, we will click on the show all files icon at the top of the **Solution Explorer** window (the icon with two papers and some dots behind them), right-click on the **References** folder, and click on **Add Reference**. We will observe on doing so that we are left with a .NET subset of assemblies that are compatible with the chosen target frameworks.

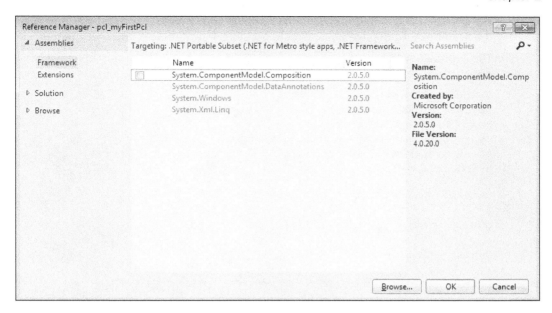

6. We will add the following lines to test the portable assembly:

```
using System;
using System.Collections.Generic;
using System.Linq;
using System.Text;

namespace pcl_myFirstPcl
{
public static class MyPortableClass
    {
public static string GetSomething()
        {
return "I am a portable class library";
        }
    }
}
```

7. Build the project.

8. Next, to try this portable assembly we could add, for example, a Silverlight project to the solution, together with an ASP.NET Web application project to wrap the Silverlight.

9. We just need to add a reference to the portable library project and add a button to the **MainPage.xaml** page that calls the portable library static method we created.

10. The code behind it should look as follows. Remember to add a `using` reference to our portable library namespace.

```
using System.Windows.Documents;
using System.Windows.Input;
using System.Windows.Media;
using System.Windows.Media.Animation;
using System.Windows.Shapes;
using pcl_myFirstPcl;

namespace SilverlightApplication_testPCL
{
public partial class MainPage : UserControl
    {
public MainPage()
        {
InitializeComponent();
        }

private void Button_Click_1(object sender, RoutedEventArgs e)
        {
            String something = MyPortableClass.GetSomething();
MessageBox.Show("Look! - I got this string from my portable class
library: " + something);
        }
    }
}
```

11. We can execute the code and check if it works.

12. In addition, we could add other types of projects, reference the Portable Library Class, and ensure that it works properly.

How it works...

We created a portable library from the **Portable Class Library** project template and selected the target frameworks.

We saw the references; note that it reinforces the visibility of the assemblies that break the compatibility with the targeted platforms, helping us to avoid mistakes.

Next we added some code, a target reference application that referenced the portable class, and used it.

There's more...

We should be aware that when deploying a .NET app that references a Portable Class Library assembly, we must specify its dependency to the correct version of the .NET Framework, ensuring that the required version is installed.

A very common and interesting usage of the Portable Class Library would be to implement MVVM. For example, we could put the View Model and Model classes inside a portable library and share it with Windows Store apps, Silverlight, and Windows Phone applications. The architecture is described in the following diagram, which has been taken from MSDN (http://msdn.microsoft.com/en-us/library/hh563947%28v=vs.110%29.aspx):

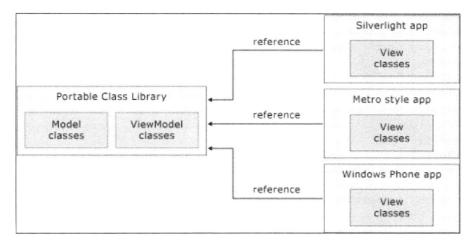

It is really interesting that the list of target frameworks is not limited and we even have a link to install additional frameworks, so I guess that the number of target frameworks will eventually grow.

Controlling the timeout in regular expressions

.NET 4.5 gives us improved control on the resolution of regular expressions so we can react when they don't resolve on time. This is extremely useful if we don't control the regular expressions/patterns, such as the ones provided by the users.

A badly formed pattern can have bad performance due to excessive backtracking and this new feature is really a lifesaver.

How to do it...

Next we are going to control the timeout in the regular expression, where we will react if the operation takes more than 1 millisecond:

1. Create a new Visual Studio project of type Console Application, named `caRegexTimeout`.

2. Open the **Program.cs** file and add a `using` clause for using regular expressions:

    ```
    Using System.Text.RegularExpressions;
    ```

3. Add the following method and call it from the `Main` function:

    ```
    private static void ExecuteRegexExpression() {
    bool RegExIsMatch = false;
    string testString = "One Tile to rule them all, One Tile to find
    them... ";
    string RegExPattern = @"([a-z ]+)*!";
    TimeSpantsRegexTimeout = TimeSpan.FromMilliseconds(1);

    try
        {
    RegExIsMatch = Regex.IsMatch(testString, RegExPattern,
    RegexOptions.None, tsRegexTimeout);
        }
    catch (RegexMatchTimeoutException ex)
        {
    Console.WriteLine("Timeout!!");
    Console.WriteLine("- Timeout specified: " + ex.MatchTimeout);
        }
    catch (ArgumentOutOfRangeException ex)
        {
    Console.WriteLine("ArgumentOutOfRangeException!!");
    Console.WriteLine(ex.Message);
        }
    Console.WriteLine("Finished succesfully: " + RegExIsMatch.
    ToString());
    Console.ReadLine();
    }
    ```

4. If we execute it, we will see that it doesn't finish successfully, showing us some details in the console window.

5. Next, we will change testString and RegExPattern to:

    ```
    String testString = "jose@brainsiders.com";
    String RegExPattern = @"^([\w-\.]+)@([\w-\.]+)\.[a-zA-Z]{2,4}$";
    ```

6. If we run it, we will now see that it runs and finishes successfully.

How it works...

The RegEx.IsMatch() method now accepts a parameter, which is matchTimeout of type TimeSpan, indicating the maximum time that we allow for the matching operation. If the execution time exceeds this amount, RegexMatchTimeoutException is launched.

In our code, we have captured it with a try-catch statement to provide a custom message and of course to react upon a badly formed regex pattern taking too much time.

We have tested it with an expression that will take some more time to validate and we got the timeout. When we changed the expression to a good one with a better execution time, the timeout was not reached.

Additionally, we also watched out for the ArgumentOutOfRangeException, which is thrown when TimeSpan is zero, or negative, or greater than 24 days.

There'smore...

We could also set a global matchTimeout for the application through the "REGEX_DEFAULT_MATCH_TIMEOUT" property with the AppDomain.SetData method:

```
AppDomain.CurrentDomain.SetData("REGEX_DEFAULT_MATCH_
TIMEOUT",TimeSpan.FromMilliseconds(200));
```

Anyway, if we specify the matchTimeout parameter, we will override the global value.

Defining the culture for an application domain

With .NET 4.5, we have in our hands a way of specifying the default culture for all of our application threads in a quick and efficient way.

How to do it...

We will now define the default culture for our application domain as follows:

1. Create a new Visual Studio project of type Console Application named `caCultureAppDomain`.

2. Open the **Program.cs** file and add the `using` clause for globalization:

   ```
   using System.Globalization;
   ```

3. Next, add the following methods:

   ```
   static void DefineAppDomainCulture() {
   String CultureString = "en-US";
   DisplayCulture();
   CultureInfo.DefaultThreadCurrentCulture = CultureInfo.CreateSpecif
   icCulture(CultureString);
   CultureInfo.DefaultThreadCurrentUICulture = CultureInfo.CreateSpec
   ificCulture(CultureString);
   DisplayCulture();
   Console.ReadLine();
   }

   static void DisplayCulture() {
   Console.WriteLine("App Domain........: {0}", AppDomain.
   CurrentDomain.Id);
   Console.WriteLine("Default Culture...: {0}", CultureInfo.
   DefaultThreadCurrentCulture);
   Console.WriteLine("Default UI Culture: {0}", CultureInfo.
   DefaultThreadCurrentUICulture);
   }
   ```

4. Then add a call to the `DefineAppDomainCulture()` method.

5. If we execute it, we will observe that the initial default cultures are null and we specify them to become the default for the App Domain.

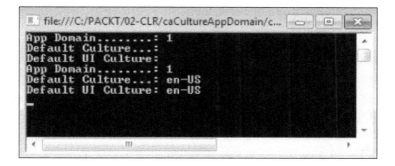

How it works...

We used the `CultureInfo` class to specify the culture and the UI of the application domain and all its threads. This is easily done through the `DefaultThreadCurrentCulture` and `DefaultThreadCurrentUICulture` properties.

There's more...

We must be aware that these properties affect only the current application domain, and if it changes we should control them.

Overriding the default reflection behavior

One interesting capability of .NET 4.5 is that we can customize our reflection context, overriding the default reflection behavior with the `CustomReflectionContext` class.

With it, we can control what properties and attributes are exposed by a class through reflection.

How to do it...

Here we will override the reflection behavior to provide additional attributes:

1. Create a new Visual Studio project of type Console Application named `caOverridingReflection`.

2. In the **References** folder of the project, in the **Solution Explorer**, add a reference to the `System.Reflection.Context` assembly.

3. Open the **Program.cs** file and add a `using` clause for system.reflection.

   ```
   using System.Reflection;
   ```

4. Next, add the `SomeClass` declaration:

```
class SomeClass
{
    //Nothing here..
}
```

5. Then add a method to visualize, through reflection, the attributes of a type:

```
public static void ShowAttributes(Type t)
{
  foreach (Attribute a in t.GetCustomAttributes())
    {
      Console.WriteLine(a);
    }
    Console.ReadLine();
}
```

6. Call it from the `Main` method and the result should be none, that is, our class has no attributes so there is nothing to display on the console.

7. Next, add a class with the name `MyCustomReflectionContext.cs` and add a reference to `System.Reflection` and `System.Reflection.Context`.

```
using System.Reflection;
using System.Reflection.Context;
```

8. Change the generated code for the following one:

```
class MyCustomReflectionContext :CustomReflectionContext
{
  protected override IEnumerable<object>
  GetCustomAttributes(MemberInfo member, IEnumerable<object>
  declaredAttributes)
    {
      if (member == typeof(SomeClass)){
          List<object>CustomAttributes = new List<object>();
          CustomAttributes.Add
          (new DefaultMemberAttribute("One"));
          CustomAttributes.Add
          (new DefaultMemberAttribute("Two"));
          CustomAttributes.Add
          (new DefaultMemberAttribute("Three"));

      return base.GetCustomAttributes
      ( member, declaredAttributes);
    }
}
```

9. Change the `ShowAttributes` method as follows:

```
public static void ShowAttributes(Type t)
{
foreach (Attribute a in t.GetCustomAttributes())
```

```
    {
        Console.WriteLine(a + " - " + (a as DefaultMemberAttribute).
        MemberName );
    }
Console.ReadLine();
}
```

10. Finally, change the code in the `Main` method as follows so that we can test it properly:

```
static void Main(string[] args)
{
Console.WriteLine("1. Without Custom Reflection Context");
ShowAttributes(typeof(SomeClass));

Console.WriteLine("2. With Custom Reflection Context");
MyCustomReflectionContextCustRefCtx = new
MyCustomReflectionContext();
Type Mappedtype = CustRefCtx.MapType(typeof(SomeClass).
GetTypeInfo());
ShowAttributes(Mappedtype);
}
```

11. If we execute the code, we will get the result shown in the following screenshot:

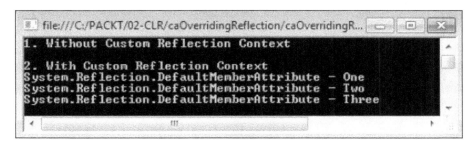

How it works...

We used reflection to get the custom attributes of a type we just created and we got none.

Next, we created a `CustomReflectionContext` that will allow us to customize what is exposed through reflection. In our case, we are ensuring that if the class is our recently created class, it should return three `DefaultMemberAttribute` replies. If not, it will return the current attributes of the class.

To illustrate this reflection context, create an instance of the reflection context to map a concrete type, SomeClass in our case. We will now have this new mapped type created in the reflection context and thus affected by it.

Finally, we used reflection as we did previously but now we will get three new attributes that we did not get before.

There's more...

With .NET 4.5, we can customize the reflection output of types as we see fit, as it is able to provide virtualized type information. This can be useful in many situations when we want more flexibility in providing type-driven behaviors or to dynamically change the properties that we want to make available.

We had TypeDescriptors and PropertyDescriptors before but they were not really a solution for design time, which CustomReflectionContext is.

A smart application of this would be to get the MEF to compose types that aren't MEF-enabled (that is, decorated with the MEF attributes). When constructing catalogs specifying ReflectionContext, MEF will project types through that reflection context and use the resulting view for its composition mechanism.

 This next great application suggestion is from Mircea Trofin, from the CLR product team–thanks, Mircea!

Using the new ZipArchive class

We have two new classes, ZipArchive and ZipArchiveEntry, which add the capability to create .zip archives to the .NET framework. This was possible previously, but with several limitations.

How to do it...

Next we will see how to use the ZipArchive class to create a Zip file and to extract it to a concrete location.

1. Create a new Visual Studio project of type Console Application named caZipArchive.

2. Add the System.IO.Compression and System.IO.Compression.Filesystem assemblies as references to the project.

3. Open the **Program.cs** file and add the following `using` clauses:

```
using System.IO;
using System.IO.Compression;
```

4. Next, add the following method:

```
static void CreateZipFile() {

    String ZipPath= @"C:\PACKT\02-CLR\caZipArchive\test\";
    String ZipFilePath = ZipPath + "test.zip";
    String FileName01 = "OneTextDocument.txt";
    String FileName02 = "OtherTextDocument.txt";
    String FileToZip01 = ZipPath + FileName01;
    String FileToZip02 = ZipPath + FileName02;

using (FileStreamZipToOpen = new FileStream(ZipFilePath, FileMode.
CreateNew))
    {
     using (ZipArchiveZArchive = new ZipArchive(ZipToOpen,
     ZipArchiveMode.Create))
       {
        ZArchive.CreateEntryFromFile(FileToZip01, FileName01);
        ZArchive.CreateEntryFromFile(FileToZip02, FileName02);
        }
    }
}
```

5. We should change the directory address and create the two files at the corresponding folder, just for testing purposes.

6. Call it from the `Main` method and execute the application. We should see that a Zip file has been created for us.

7. Delete the Zip File.

8. Add the following method:

```
static void ExtractZipFile() {
    String ZipPath = @"C:\PACKT\02-CLR\caZipArchive\test\";
    String ZipFilePath = ZipPath + "test.zip";
    String ExtractionPath = @"C:\PACKT\02-CLR\caZipArchive\test\
unzip";

using (ZipArchiveZArchive = ZipFile.OpenRead(ZipFilePath))
    {
```

```
foreach (ZipArchiveEntry zaEntry in ZArchive.Entries)
        {
    zaEntry.ExtractToFile(Path.Combine(ExtractionPath,
    zaEntry.FullName));
        }
    }
}
```

9. And call it in the `Main` method, just after `CreateZipFile`:

```
static void Main(string[] args)
{
    //First we create the zip file
CreateZipFile();

    //Next, we extract it
ExtractZipFile();
}
```

10. Delete the previously generated ZIP file and create the unzip directory.

11. If we execute the application, a ZIP file should be generated on the specified directory, and we should find all the files that we added in the extraction directory.

How it works...

We used `FileStream` to create a new file stream and write to it with `ZipArchive`.

Additionally, we added two files using the `CreateEntryFromFile` extension method of the `ZipArchive` class that is the result of adding the `System.IO.Compression.FileSystem` assembly.

With this we had our ZIP file created.

Continuing, we opened our ZIP file using the `OpenRead` method of the `ZipFile` class, which returns a `ZipArchive` object that represents the package of compressed files.

We can iterate all the entries with a simple `foreach` instruction. For each `ZipArchiveEntry`, we extract it with the `ExtractToFile` extension method.

And that's it! In a few lines of code we have created a ZIP file, added some files, and then extracted the ZIP files to another folder.

There's more...

We could also specify the level of compression, edit the files within the ZIP file, or update existing ZIP files.

Additionally, for simplicity we 'neither validated for the existence of files or directories nor checked for any errors, so we should do this properly in a production environment.

We should be aware that the extension methods (provided by the `System.IO.Compression. FileSystem` assembly) that we used aren't available in Windows Store apps. There we should compress and decompress using the `GZipStream` or `DeflateStream` class.

Understanding async and await in .NET 4.5

The new asynchronous capabilities of .NET 4.5 rely on the `async` and `await` modifiers. Basically we have two important points here:

▶ The async modifier indicates to the compiler that a method or lambda expression is asynchronous—we call them async methods.

▶ The `await` operator, which can only be used within an async method, is applied to a task to suspend execution of the method until the task is complete. Meanwhile, the control is returned to the caller of that method.

How to do it...

Here we will use the `async` and `await` features in a basic way to clearly understand them.

1. Create a new Visual Studio project of type Console Application named `caAsyncAwait`.

2. Add a reference to the `System.Net.Http` assembly.

3. In the `Program.cs` file, add the following `using` clauses:

```
using System.Net;
using System.IO;
```

4. Next, add the following methods:

```
Static async Task HttpTestAsync(String url) {
byte[] result = await GetURLContentsAsync(url);
Console.WriteLine("Received {0,8} bytes..", result.Length);
}
private static async Task<byte[]> GetURLContentsAsync(string url)
```

```
{
var content = new MemoryStream();
var webReq = (HttpWebRequest)WebRequest.Create(url);
using (WebResponse response = await webReq.GetResponseAsync())
    {
    using (Stream responseStream = response.GetResponseStream())
        {
        Await responseStream.CopyToAsync(content);
        }
    }
Return content.ToArray();
}
```

5. Add a call to the `HttpTestAsync` function in the `Main` method surrounded with some sentences in the `Console.Writeline` method to keep track of what is happening:

```
static void Main(string[] args)
{
Console.WriteLine("Start of Main Method");
HttpTestAsync("http://www.packtpub.com/forthcoming-titles");
Console.WriteLine("End of Main Metod");

Console.ReadLine();
}
```

6. We should execute the application and get the results shown in the following screenshot:

7. Next, add the following method:

```
Static async void MultipleHttpTestAsync()
{
    Task t1 = HttpTestAsync("http://www.packtpub.com/forthcoming-
    titles");
    Task t2 = HttpTestAsync("http://www.silverlightguy.com");
    Task t3 = HttpTestAsync("http://www.microsoft.com");
```

```
await t1;
await t2;
await t3;

Console.WriteLine("All tasks have finished..");
}
```

8. Comment the previous call to `HttpTestAsync` in the `Main` method and next to it add a call to `MultipleHttpTestAsync`.

9. If we execute the code, we will see that the different tasks are executed after the `Main` method ends. If we execute it several times, their finishing order might change.

10. Now, we will add a similar method:

```
Static async void OptimizedMultipleHttpTestAsync()
{
    Task t3 = HttpTestAsync("http://www.packtpub.com/forthcoming-
    titles");
    Task t2 = HttpTestAsync("http://www.silverlightguy.com");
    Task t1 = HttpTestAsync("http://www.microsoft.com");

    Task[] tasklist= new Task[] { t1, t2, t3 };
    Await Task.WhenAll(tasklist);

    Console.WriteLine("All tasks have finished..");
}
```

11. Then we will change the call from the `Main` method to this new method.

12. If we execute it, we get practically the same output as with the previous code.

How it works...

We have initially created the `HttpTestAsync` method, adding to it the async modifier, which indicates that the method (or the lambda expression) is asynchronous. These methods are called async methods.

An async method provides the ability to be called without blocking the caller's thread, which is convenient for long-running jobs. Also, the caller of an async method resumes its work without waiting for the async method to finish, unless we indicate in the call to the async method that we wish to wait until it finishes; we will do that with the `await` expression.

The `await` operator is applied to a task in an asynchronous method to suspend the execution of the method until the awaited task is completed. Basically, it waits for the completion of the task. Nowadays, the thread is not blocked and the process continues, but the rest of the code after the `await` operator becomes an automatic callback method.

It is obvious that the task where the `await` operator is applied must be modified by the async modifier and returns a task or task of TResult, that is, when the task is returned by an async method, it might not be the source of the task.

Additionally, by convention, all asynchronous method names should end in `Async`.

Going back to the `HttpTestAsync` method we just commented, we have marked it as async and it is returning a task that we can wait for with the `await` operator. Inside it, because it is an async method, it can await the completion of the `GetURLContentsAsync` method.

The `GetURLContentsAsync` method is an async method that retrieves a URL with a `WebRequest` method, gets its content as a response, and returns it when it is finished.

`HttpTestAsync` takes the resultant content from `GetURLContentsAsync` as we are waiting for it to finish with await and writes on the console the total amount of bytes received.

We execute the first test with the following lines of code:

```
Console.WriteLine("Start of Main Method");
HttpTestAsync("http://www.packtpub.com/forthcoming-titles");
Console.WriteLine("End of Main Metod");
```

We continue with the `Main` method before the awaited `GetURLContentsAsync` method finishes so that the main console writelines are written first.

In the next example we code, `MultipleHttpTestAsync`, we are creating three tasks to download three URLs asynchronously and then we await them. The tasks are being executed in parallel since they are started at creation. The `await` expression only indicates that the processing can't continue until the task finishes.

So with this code, we really are controlling the start time of the tasks (that is, the async methods are called) but not their end time. The order of the `await` operators can affect the times a bit but they might finish before arriving at the `await` expressions:

```
Task t3 = HttpTestAsync("http://www.packtpub.com/forthcoming-titles");
Task t2 = HttpTestAsync("http://www.silverlightguy.com");
Task t1 = HttpTestAsync("http://www.microsoft.com");

await t1;
await t2;
await t3;
```

A more elegant solution is what we will do in the next example, where we add all the tasks to an array and use the `Task.WhenAll` method on this generated collection of tasks:

```
Task[] tasklist = new Task[] { t1, t2, t3 };
await Task.WhenAll(tasklist);
```

This method asynchronously awaits multiple asynchronous operations that it expects as an IEnumerable of tasks.

This way the code will resume when all the tasks have been completed, not before or after.

There's more...

We have seen the basics of `async` and `await`, explored task handling, and even executed some the tasks in parallel. We ended up using a method from the `Task` class, `WhenAll`, which enabled us to wait for a list of tasks to finish.

But there is a lot more to explore with task management, which you will be familiar with if you have already explored the TPL. We have plenty of options there to control the processing flow of our application in ways that would have been extremely complicated earlier.

Using the new asynchronous file I/O operations

There are some brand new asynchronous methods for file operation I/O, which are clearly designed for providing resource-intensive work without blocking the main UI thread.

For I/O operations, we have some interesting methods such as `ReadAsync`, `WriteAsync`, `CopyToAsync`, `FlushAsync`, `ReadLineAsync`, and `ReadToEndasync`, which are implemented on stream classes and on classes that read and/or write to streams such as `TextWriter` or `TextReader`.

How to do it...

Next we will see a simple example that we can extrapolate to a majority of these methods with ease.

1. Create a new Visual Studio project of type Console Application named `caAsyncIO`.

2. Add a `using` clause for `System.IO`:

```
using System.IO;
```

3. Copy the following base method:

```
Private async static void CopyFolderContents() {
String SourceFolder = @"C:\PACKT\02-CLR\caAsyncIO\source";
String DestinationFolder = @"C:\PACKT\02-CLR\caAsyncIO\
destination";

Console.WriteLine("Going to copy {0} files..", Directory.
EnumerateFiles(SourceFolder).Count());

foreach (string SourceFile in Directory.
EnumerateFiles(SourceFolder))
    {
        String DestinationFile = DestinationFolder + SourceFile.
        Substring(SourceFile.LastIndexOf('\\'));
        Await CopyFilesWithFileStreams(SourceFile,
        DestinationFile);
    }
}
```

4. Then call it from the `Main` method:

```
static void Main(string[] args)
{
CopyFolderContents();
Console.ReadLine();
}
```

5. We just need to add the `CopyFilesWithFileStreams` method:

```
Private async static Task CopyFilesWithFileStreams(StringStartFi
le, String DestinationFile)
{
    using (FileStreamSourceFileStream = File.Open(StartFile,
    FileMode.Open))
    {
        using (FileStreamDestinationFileStream = File.
        Create(DestinationFile))
```

```
        {
        Await SourceFileStream.CopyToAsync(DestinationFileStream);
        Console.WriteLine("Copied the " + DestinationFile);
        }
    }
}
```

6. Then we can execute the `FileStream` I/O test. The execution of our application should give us the following result:

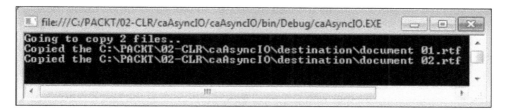

7. We will add the following two methods to implement a stream version of what we just did:

```
Private async static Task CopyFilesWithStreams(String StartFile,
String DestinationFile) {
using (StreamReader SourceStreamReader = File.OpenText(StartFile))
    {
    using (StreamWriter DestinationStreamWriter = File.
    CreateText(DestinationFile))
        {
        Await CopyFilesAsync(SourceStreamReader,
        DestinationStreamWriter);
Console.WriteLine("Copied the " + DestinationFile);
        }
    }
}
Public async static Task CopyFilesAsync(StreamReader SourceReader,
StreamWriter DestinationWriter)
{
    char[] buffer = new char[0x1000];
    int numRead;
    while ((numRead = await SourceReader.ReadAsync(buffer, 0,
    buffer.Length)) != 0)
    {
        Await DestinationWriter.WriteAsync(buffer, 0, numRead);
    }
}
```

8. We will only need to modify the `CopyFolderContents()` method by commenting the call to `CopyFilesWithFileStreams` and adding a call to `CopyFilesWithStreams`:

```
await CopyFilesWithStreams(SourceFile, DestinationFile);
```

9. If we execute it, the result will be exactly the same as before.

How it works...

We have set up a system to copy all the files from one directory to another. Using the `Directory.EnumerateFiles` method does the trick, and we just have to enumerate them and delegate the task to a `copy` method with source and destination paths that include the filename.

Additionally, `CopyFolderContents` has been declared async so we can use the `await` operator inside it, and we do that with `CopyFilesWithStreams`, the first method we implement to read and copy the file using `FileStream` objects. We do it with nested `using`, the first for opening the file with `File.Open` and the second for creating and writing the destination file with `File.Create`.

Finally we use the `CopyToASync` asynchronous method to do the trick. Of course, we use the `await` operator inside it.

Next, we implement the same functionality but with the `StreamReader` and `StreamWriter` objects. We do it in a similar way, that is, with the two nested `using` clauses, one for the reader and the other for the writer.

For executing the reading and writing tasks, we implemented our own method that executes a while loop that reads and writes a buffer from the source stream into the destination stream until it finishes copying. For doing this, it uses the new `ReadAsync` and `WriteAsync` methods.

There's more...

We have seen how to use some of the many available methods, and there are many more to explore, but anyway, the concepts and workings are similar to those we have just seen.

See also

▶ The *Understanding async and await in .NET 4.5* recipe.

3
Understanding the New Networking Capabilities

In this chapter, we will cover how to use the `HttpClient` and new `System.Net.Http` namespaces.

Introduction

.NET 4.5 brings improved capabilities in networking such as more support for internationalization, protocol improvements, better performance, and new programming interfaces for HTTP and WebSockets. The main improvement is that it now fully supports WebSockets and the complete HTTP standard.

.NET Framework 4.5 enhances internationalization with the following features:

- **Internationalized Domain Name** (**IDN**) support
- **E-mail Address Internationalization** (**EAI**) support
- International **Uniform Resource Identifier** (**URI**) support, compliant with the latest RFCs from the **Internet Engineering Task Force** (**IETF**)

Regarding protocol support, the additions are:

- Better IPv6 support
- Improved Sockets protocol support with a dual-mode socket support

As for new namespaces, we now have `System.Net.Http`, `System.Net.Http.Headers`, and `System.Net.WebSockets` namespaces. We have improvements on classes such as `HttpListener`, `Uri`, `Socket`, and on namespaces such as `System.Net.Mail` or `System.Net.NetworkInformation`.

We will now explore in practice some of these features to get a solid grasp on the new capabilities.

Using the HttpClient and the new System. Net.Http namespaces

`HttpClient` is a new .NET 4.5 class using the HTTP protocol, similar to `WebClient` or `HttpWebRequest`. A highlight of this class is the full support of Async.

In fact it's not such a novelty, since we already had it on the REST Starter Kit and the implementation of the .NET 4.0 Web API.

The `HttpClient` class resides on the `System.Net.Http` namespace, which is a brand new .NET 4.5 namespace. Basically, we use `HttpClient` to create HTTP requests, manage the response, and process the response's content.

Some of the most interesting capabilities are:

 ▸ Helper methods that create requests and process the responses
 ▸ The possibility of defining a default header to apply to all sent messages
 ▸ Timeout and cancellation management

Getting ready

In order to use this recipe you should have Visual Studio 2012 installed.

How to do it...

Here we will create a basic application that exemplifies the clear usage of `HTTPClient`:

1. First open Visual Studio 2012 and create a new project. We will select the **Console Application** template from the visual C# category and name it `caHttpClient`.

2. Add a reference to the `System.Net.Http` assembly.

3. Open `Program.cs` and add a `using` clause to the added assembly namespace:

   ```
   using System.Net.Http;
   ```

4. Add the following method to perform a basic test of the new `HttpClient` class:

```
private static async Task TestHttpClient() {
try
    {
    HttpClient HttpCli = new HttpClient();

    Console.WriteLine("Executing the Asyncronous http petition ");
    HttpResponse MessageHttpResponse = await HttpCli.
    GetAsync("http://www.packtpub.com/");
    HttpResponse.EnsureSuccessStatusCode();
    string StringHttpResponse = await HttpResponse.Content.
    ReadAsStringAsync();

    Console.WriteLine(StringHttpResponse);
    }
catch (HttpRequestException e)
    {
    Console.WriteLine("\nThere was a problem..");
    Console.WriteLine("Problem :{0} ", e.Message);
    }
}
```

And call it from the `Main` method:

```
static void Main(string[] args)
{
Console.WriteLine("Press a key to start ");
Console.ReadLine();

TestHttpClient();

Console.ReadLine();
}
```

5. If we execute it, we will get the following result:

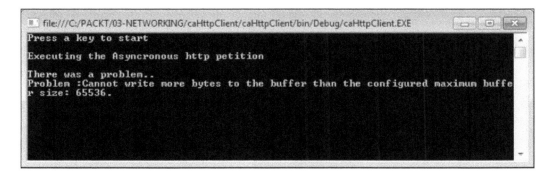

6. So we just have to increase the size of the response buffer.

7. Before executing the HTTP petition, we will increase it with the following line:

```
HttpCli.MaxResponseContentBufferSize = 512000;
```

8. You can put in any value, but it is a common issue that the value entered is too small, so increasing the default response buffer is highly recommended, as we just did in the previous step.

9. Next we will open the NuGet package manager by navigating to **Tools | Library Package Manager | Manage NuGet Packages for Solution...**.

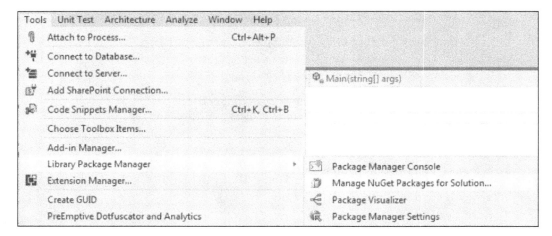

10. Once in the NuGet Package manager, locate and add the **Microsoft ASP.NET Web API Client Libraries** package. Adding this to our project will add the needed references, `System.Net.Http.Formatting`, `System.Net.Http`, and `Newtonsoft.Json`.

11. Add a using clause for the `Newtonsoft.Json` namespace and the following method:

```csharp
private static async Task TestHttpClientJson()
{
try
    {
HttpClient HttpCli = new HttpClient();

HttpResponseMessage response = await HttpCli.GetAsync("http://api.
worldbank.org/countries?format=json");
response.EnsureSuccessStatusCode();

JArray content = await response.Content.ReadAsAsync<JArray>();
return Console.WriteLine("First 10 World Bank countries:");
var i = 0;
foreach (var country in content[1].Take(10))
        {
i = i + 1;
Console.WriteLine(" - {0} : {1}", i, country.
Value<string>("name"));
```

```
        }
    }
catch (HttpRequestException e)
    {
    Console.WriteLine("\nThere was a problem..");
    Console.WriteLine("Problem :{0} ", e.Message);
    }
}
```

12. Add the call to this function in the `Main` method and execute the application. We should get the following result:

```
file:///F:/NET45Packt/CH03-Networking/code/caHttpClient - 02/caHttpClient/bin/Debug/caHttpCli...

Press a key to start
First 10 World Bank countries:
  - 1  : Aruba
  - 2  : Afghanistan
  - 3  : Angola
  - 4  : Albania
  - 5  : Andorra
  - 6  : Arab World
  - 7  : United Arab Emirates
  - 8  : Argentina
  - 9  : Armenia
  - 10 : American Samoa
```

How it works...

We created a console application and added the `System.Net.Http` assemblies and namespaces.

Then, we created an instance of the `HttpClient` class, extended its maximum buffer size, and instanced a `HttpResponseMessage` class that we used to capture the response from the `HttpClient` class.

To fill the response message, we are using the `GetAsync` method of the `HttpClient` class. It is an `Async` method, as most of the methods we can find on this namespace. It makes the code easy to read.

Alternatively, we could have used other read methods such as `ReadByteArray`, `GetStream`, or `GetStringAsync`. In fact, the helper method `GetStringAsync` could have been used as follows:

```
stringHttpStringResponse = await HttpCli.GetStringAsync(http://www.
packtpub.com/);
```

Instead of:

```
HttpResponse MessageHttpResponse = await HttpCli.GetAsync("http://www.
packtpub.com/");
HttpResponse.EnsureSuccessStatusCode();
string StringHttpResponse = await HttpResponse.Content.
ReadAsStringAsync();
```

Additionally, we get the errors and validations from the response message; in this case we use the `HttpResponseMessage` method to ensure that the response was successful and throw an error if not:

```
HttpResponse.EnsureSuccessStatusCode();
```

We are accessing the `Content` property of the `HttpResponseMessage` class to get the string value. This `Content` is of type `HttpContent` and, if needed, we could access its `Headers` property and all its related properties such as `Content-Language`, `Content-Type`, and `Last-Modified`:

```
string StringHttpResponse = await HttpResponse.Content.
ReadAsStringAsync();
```

Next, we write the content we got, in this case, our website's HTML content.

Additionally, we have expanded our basic `hello HttpClient` by adding in some extension methods provided by `System.Net.Http.Formatting` and some JSON built into .NET with `Newtonsoft.Json`, both of them added with the **Microsoft ASP.NET Web API Client Libraries** NuGet package.

`System.Net.Http.Formatting` provides us with support for serialization, deserialization, and some other features on top of `System.Net.Http`.

`Newtonsoft.Json` enhances JSON helper objects with functionalities to read and manipulate JSON documents such as `JsonArray` and `JsonToken`.

In this example, we get a URI that returns JSON data, and retrieve it with `GetAsync` into an `HttpResponseMessage` object:

```
HttpResponseMessage response = await HttpCli.GetAsync("http://api.
worldbank.org/countries?format=json");
```

Next we read the `HttpContent` page that we got from our response message with `ReadAsAsync<JArray>()`:

```
JArraycontent = await response.Content.ReadAsAsync<JArray>();
```

This does the magic and we now have an array of `JsonToken` elements that we can iterate through and write into the console.

There's more...

By now, we should have a grasp of the power of `HttpClient` and its related assemblies, but there's more than what we have seen.

`HttpClient` provides us with a powerful API to access everything exposed through HTTP via `GET`, `POST`, `PUT`, and `DELETE`, which support the standard very well and also nicely match the WebAPI on the server side.

4

Understanding the new features of Entity Framework 5.0

In this chapter we will cover:

- ▶ Creating our first Code First application
- ▶ Using Code First Migrations

Introduction

Entity Framework (EF) has really grown, and with .NET 4.5, we have a mature framework that has some new capabilities, such as Code First Migrations, which we will explore in the following recipes.

Note that we will do that in a progressive way, so we will be creating a base for some of the recipes in the next chapter.

Creating our first "Code First" application

Our first application will create a database from code. We will start by creating an ASP.NET project that we will reuse in the following recipes.

Getting ready

In order to use this recipe, you should have Visual Studio 2012 installed.

How to do it...

Here we will create a Code First application and see the main concepts behind this technology and how to use it properly.

1. First open Visual Studio 2012 and create a new project. We will select the **ASP.NET MVC 4 Web Application** template from **Visual C#** | **Web** and name it EFCodeFirst as shown in the following screenshot:

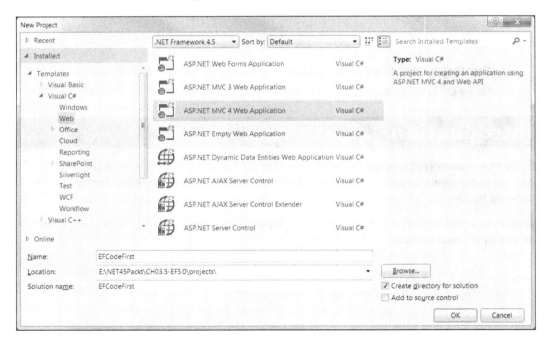

2. Select the **Internet Application** template as shown in the following screenshot:

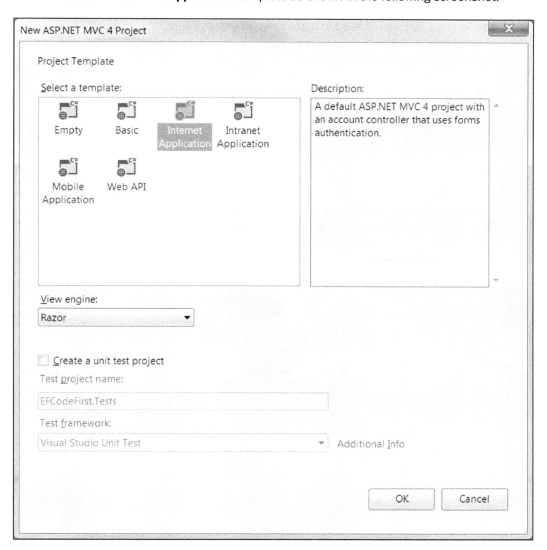

3. Next, we will create a class that we will use as the schema to create a table. We will add the `BookModel` class to the `Models` folder of our project as shown in the following code. Note that we will need to add a reference to `System.ComponentModel.DataAnnotations`.

```
namespace EFCodeFirst.Model
{
    public class BookModel
    {
        [Required]
        public int Id { get; set; }
        public String Title { get; set; }
        public String Description { get; set; }
    }
}
```

4. In order to ensure we have the **EntityFramework NuGet** package, as shown in the following screenshot, we will right-click on the project and select the **Manage NuGet Packages...** option and validate that we have the **EntityFramework** package selected; if not, we will install it.

We will build the project before continuing, so that everything is up-to-date. If not, we will not be able to see the classes we just created in the template dialog.

5. Right-click on the **Controllers** folder and select **Add | Controller...** as shown in the following screenshot:

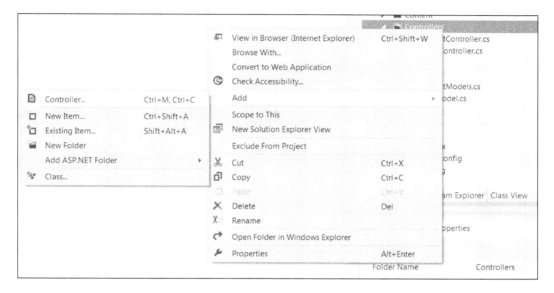

6. On the **Add Controller** dialogue that appears, we will name the controller `BooksController`.

7. On the next field, we will select the option **MVC Controller with read/write actions and views, using Entity Framework**.

8. Continuing, at the **Model class** option we will choose the **BookModel** class we just created.

9. At the **Data context class** option we will select the **<New Data Context>** option and enter the name `EFCodeFirst.Models.BooksContext` and click on the **OK** button. The dialog should look as follows:

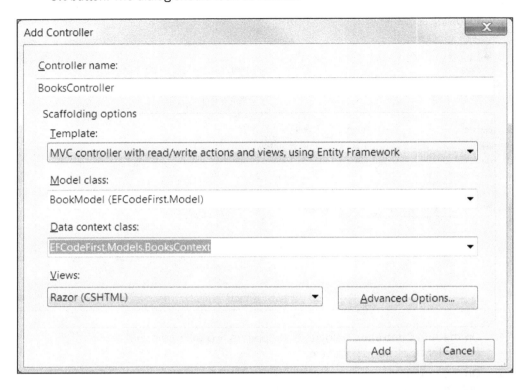

10. We will press the **Add** button displayed in the previous screenshot.

    As a result, the `BooksController.cs` and `BooksContext.cs` files will be added with methods to handle data, together with a `view` folder containing some files for each needed view.

11. We will open the `BooksContext` file to see how simple it would be to create this class on our own, should we need it for other projects without the autogeneration help that this tooling provides:

```
public class BooksContext : DbContext
{
    // You can add custom code to this file. Changes will not be
overwritten.
```

```
        //
        // If you want Entity Framework to drop and regenerate your
database
        // automatically whenever you change your model schema, add
the following
        // code to the Application_Start method in your Global.asax
file.
        // Note: this will destroy and re-create your database with
every model change.
        //
        // System.Data.Entity.Database.SetInitializer(new System.
Data.Entity.DropCreateDatabaseIfModelChanges<EFCodeFirst.Models.
BooksContext>());

        public BooksContext() : base("name=BooksContext")
        {
        }

        public DbSet<BookModel> BookModels { get; set; }
    }
```

12. Finally, we should be able to run the application by adding /books to our URI, for
    instance http://localhost:5049/books, so that we can start creating our
    book collection as shown in the following screenshot:

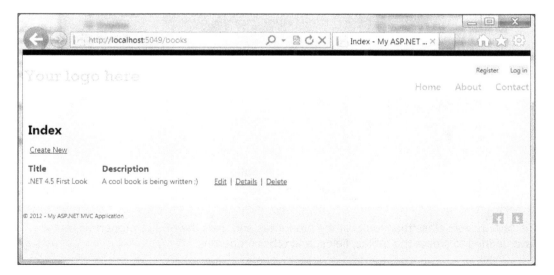

How it works...

We created an ASP.NET application as a placeholder to showcase the EF capabilities, but we could have chosen other options, such as a console application.

The first step was creating a basic class with some properties that we want to use to create a database table. Continuing, we validated that we had the **EntityFramework NuGet** package so that we could properly work with EF Code First.

Next, we added a controller that was automatically created for our `BooksModel` class, creating all of the tools that are necessary for MVC to work with the data. This automates for us the creation of the data context for the `DbContext` base class.

Additionally, in the `BooksContext.cs` file we can observe that we have a reference to the `System.Data.Entity` namespace. If we were to create this manually, we would also need to add this reference manually. This context is all the code we need to store and retrieve data; a `DbSet` property of the entity type inside this context class is shown in the following code:

```
public DbSet<BookModel> BookModels { get; set; }
```

Of course, we will need to create an instance of the context class, which `DbContext` will use to create a `LocalDB` database for us (this is installed by default by Visual Studio 2012). The database is named after the fully qualified name of our context, as we can see in the following screenshot:

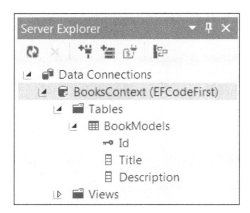

The `DbContext` class then looks at the properties and uses the `DbSet` properties that we have defined to create the tables, fields, and other properties.

There's more...

We have just grasped the power of Entity Framework Code First, but there's much more than we have seen.

This release is especially powerful in its ability to deal with model changes, and with it we can go ahead or back in time in a proper way. We will see how this works in the next recipe.

We have the Code First conventions that EF uses to discover the model, which are type discovery, primary key, relationship, complex types, and connection string, explained in the following list:

- ▶ **Type discovery**: This convention is used to create the database representation of our model, pulling also any referenced types. If we created a `BookComments` class and referenced it from our `BookModel` class, it would be included automatically.

- ▶ **Primary key**: This is a convention that determines that a property is a primary key if it contains the `id` or `ID` string, mapping them as an integer identity column.

- ▶ **Relationship**: This is a convention that infers relationships based on the navigation properties of our class. An example of this would be having the previously mentioned reference to the `BookComment` class set as:

```
public virtual ICollection<BookComment> BookComments {get; set;}
```

- ▶ **Complex types**: This is a convention that determines that a class with no detected primary key that does not reference other entities is a complex type.

- ▶ **Connection string**: This is a convention that creates the database on the `LocalDB` Server, naming it after the fully qualified name of the context.

The Code First conventions can be extended by Data Annotations, which are attributes that enable further configuration. Among other things, we can identify a field as a key or foreign key or mark that a field is required, as we did in our `BookModel` class. Note that we, in practice, override almost all of the conventions with these Data Annotation attributes.

For example, it would be clearer if, in our class, we put the `[Key]` attribute in our key field:

```
[Key]
public int Id { get; set; }
```

These Data Annotations are useful to supplement the conventions or to directly override them.

We also have a fluent API, which gets us into the advanced part of Code First, and thus it is recommended that we use it only in those situations where Data Annotations can't help us. With fluent API, we can override the `OnModelCreating` method in the `DbContext` base class and configure the properties with more capabilities than with the conventions or Data Annotations model.

Of course we can use all these models combined in any way we wish, getting the best of all worlds.

See also

Following the next recipe is recommended, since it is really important to get a solid comprehension of how Code First and Code First Migrations are used.

Additionally, I do recommend that you explore the topics, EF's conventions, Data Annotations, and fluent API.

Using Code First Migrations

In this recipe we will use Code First code Migrations to evolve our model and update the database. You might be asking yourself why this is so important. Isn't this just another way of doing something we already knew how to do?

Not so! It solves a very important problem in a simple and efficient way. Haven't we all at some time had the problem of deploying software and keeping the database up-to-date? Well, this solves this exact problem. And in a very easy and simple way, I must add.

How? Keep reading.

Getting ready

In order to use this recipe, you should have Visual Studio 2012 installed. It would be good to have implemented the previous recipe and worked on the resulting solution.

How to do it...

Using this recipe we will implement Code First Migrations and show how to evolve our model and revert it to a previous version.

First, open Visual Studio 2012 and open the previous project. We recommend copying it to a new folder so if anything goes wrong (you all know Murphy is always present) we can start a new one.

Change the project name to `EFCodeFirstMigrations`.

We will start by enabling migrations. To do this, we will open the **Package Manager Console** option and type the `Enable-Migrations` command into it, pressing **Return** to execute it. We will observe that a `Migrations` folder has been created in the project with two source files, one for the initial creation of the database and the other for the configuration (`configuration.cs`).

We will open the `configuration.cs` file and change the `AutomaticMigrationsEnabled` property's value to `true` using the following line of code:

```
AutomaticMigrationsEnabled = true
```

Note that we could have enabled Automatic Migrations with this command:

```
Enable-Migrations - EnableAutomaticMigrations
```

Let's add a minor change to our `BookModel` class to see how this works out. We will add a Boolean property named `IsOnSale` as shown in the following code line:

```
public boolIsOnSale {get; set;}
```

Apply the pending changes from our code to the database with the command `Update-Database` that we will type into and execute with the **Package Manager Console**. If we want more details on what is happening, we can also execute this command with the `-Verbose` flag as shown in the following code line:

```
Update-Database -Verbose
```

It would be good to validate that our database has been properly generated, so we should open our **Server Explorer** panel and refresh it to reflect the changes.

Next, we will comment the added property and execute the `Update-Database` command again. It will not be executed because it would result in data loss.

We will uncomment the `IsOnSale` property and add a `BookRating` integer property to the `BookModel` class.

For medium to advanced scenarios for which we want more control over what happens, we have Code Migrations. We will enable it by going to our `configuration.cs` file and setting the `AutomaticMigrationsEnabled` property to `false`.

Then we will go to our **Package Manager Console** and execute the `Add-Migration` command, followed by the name we want to give to this code migration. We will use the name `BookRating` as it describes very well what this migration will do.

Now a new file has appeared in our `Migrations` folder, named `BookRating.cs`, prefixed with a timestamp that will help us with the ordering. If we open it, we will clearly see and understand how it works:

```
public partial class BookRating : DbMigration
{
    public override void Up()
    {
```

```
AddColumn("dbo.BookModels", "BookRating", c =>c.Int
(nullable: false));
}

public override void Down()
{
DropColumn("dbo.BookModels", "BookRating");
}
}
```

There we can see the `Up` and `Down` methods that will be invoked when needed. We can modify them to do what we want. For example, we will rate the books with a rating of five by default. We will modify the `AddColumn` function with the following code:

```
AddColumn("dbo.BookModels", "BookRating",
  c =>c.Int(nullable:false, defaultValue:5));
```

The only thing left now is to update the database with the `Update-Database` command. Go on and execute it.

To validate that everything has gone as expected, we should open the **Server Explorer** panel, navigate to our database, and finally, right-click on our table, selecting the **Show Table Data** option. We can appreciate that the **BookRating** column has been added and also that its value has been set to **5** as shown in the following screenshot:

	Id	Title	Description	IsOnSale	BookRating
►	1	.NET 4.5 First Look	A cool book is being written ;)	False	5
*	NULL	NULL	NULL	NULL	NULL

Now we are going to go back to the previous version. To do this, we will use the `Update-Database` command together with the `–TargetMigration` flag. We will execute the following code on the **Package Manager Console** window:

```
Update-Database -TargetMigration:"InitialCreate"
```

This will not execute properly as it will produce a loss of data. We must add the `–Force` flag to execute it without problems. Excecute the code previously mentioned, once again, but using the `–Force` flag:

```
Update-Database -TargetMigration:"InitialCreate" -Force
```

We can again update the database to the latest state with the `Update-Database -TargetMigration:"BookRating"` command. We don't have any reason to use the `-Force` flag since there will be no data loss in this case.

How it works...

We enabled Code First Migrations with the `Enable-Migrations` command and manually changed the mode to **Automatic Migrations**, showing its behavior with a simple property change.

With Automatic Migrations, we can execute the `Update-Database` command, and all is done for us, without any need to handle versions or anything else. We saw that this comes with the drawback of not being able to move to a previous version.

Continuing, we activated Code Migrations and generated a migration with the `Add-Migration` command, which, as we saw, we can use to move up and down within the different versions, and finally, we customized a bit of migration to provide a default value.

Next, we saw how to move back and forward in time to a specific migration in a very easy way and also used the `-Force` flag to enable proper downgrading in cases where the elimination of fields and/or tables is required. For this, the command is `Update-Database -TargetMigration:"MigrationName"`, followed by the `-Force` flag, if needed.

There's more...

In addition, to what we have seen, we might want to perform some activity with the data to fit the new model, such as copying data from one table to another, prepopulating the new entity with a default value, and likewise. To do this, we can execute SQL at any point in our migration, as we can see in the following code:

```
Sql("UPDATE dbo.BookModels SET BookRating = 5");
```

Additionally we can automatically generate the update script with the `-Script` flag indicating the source and the destination migrations:

```
Update-Database -Script -SourceMigration:$InitialDatabase -
TargetMigration:"BookRating"
```

Executing this would generate the necessary SQL script that we can then use to execute the migration directly on our SQL Server.

5
Understanding the New Features of ASP.NET

In this chapter, we will cover:

- ▶ Creating our first ASP.NET 4.5 Web Forms application
- ▶ Configuring our application to use unobtrusive validation
- ▶ Using Smart Tasks in the HTML editor
- ▶ Using WAI-ARIA support
- ▶ Using the Extract to User Control feature
- ▶ Using the Page Inspector feature
- ▶ Creating an asynchronous HTTP module

Introduction

ASP.NET has definitely improved with .NET 4.5, providing us with better tools, capabilities, and performance.

As far as capabilities are concerned, the three "flavors" of ASP.NET are greatly enhanced. First, the new async features of .NET 4.5 are really interesting on ASP.NET. The web is becoming more interconnected every day, so asynchronous requests (and responses) are in all aspects of our daily work. Second, we have in our hands a greatly enhanced IDE with capabilities such as intelli-sense and improved support for the latest versions of web-development languages. Third, NuGet has been improved and now provides some componentized functionality for ASP. NET, such as Modernizr, which enables compatibility between browsers enabling/disabling HTML5 capabilities, jQuery, and so on.

There is even more candy, with features such as unobtrusive validation, an AntiXSS library, and EF Code First.

All in all, it's become an even better framework for web development!

The following sections will explore, in practice, some of these features to get a solid grasp on the new functionality. We will start by creating an example application using some of the new features of ASP.NET 4.5.

Creating our first ASP.NET 4.5 Web Forms application

Web Forms is the classical programming framework of ASP.NET. Nowadays, much of the concepts and improvements we will see are common to the other development frameworks such as ASP.NET, MVC, and Web Pages.

In this recipe we will see how to work with the new capabilities of ASP.NET 4.5 by creating a Web Forms application.

Getting ready

In order to use this recipe you should have Visual Studio 2012.

How to do it...

Now, we will create a Code First ASP.NET Web Forms application that will create the database from code. We will also add some seed data.

1. First, open Visual Studio 2012 and create a new project. We will select the **ASP.NET Web Forms Application** template by going to **visual C# | Web category**, name it `wfSampleApp`, and press **OK** to create the application.

2. After the project has been created, add and open the NuGet Package Manager by going to **Tools | Library Package Manager | Manage NuGet Packages for Solution**.

3. Add the **Entity Framework** package to the project.

4. Create a folder in the project root with the name `CodeFirst`. We will put our related Code First files and models in this folder.

5. Place a new class item in the `CodeFirst` folder named `BookModel`. Add the following class definition there:

```
public class BookModel
{
    [ScaffoldColumn(false)]
    Public int Id { get; set; }

    [Required, StringLength(260)]
    [Display(Name="Title", Description="The title of the book",
    Order=1)]
    public String Title { get; set; }

    [Display(Name = "Description", Description = "The description
     of the book", Order = 2)]
    public String Description { get; set; }
    public bool IsOnSale { get; set; }
    public int BookRating { get; set; }
    public int? CategoryId { get; set; }

}
```

6. Create another model with the name of `CategoryModel` with the following code:

```
public class CategoryModel
{
    [ScaffoldColumn(false)]
    Public int Id { get; set; }

    [Required, StringLength(140)]
    [Display(Name = "Title", Description = "The title of the
    category", Order = 1)]
    public String Title { get; set; }

    [Display(Name = "Description", Description = "The description
    of the category", Order = 2)]
    public String Description { get; set; }
    public virtual ICollection<BookModel> Books { get; set; }
}
```

7. Next we will add the `Context` class in the same location. Add a `BooksContext.cs` class with the following code in it:

```
public class BooksContext : DbContext
{
Public DbSet<BookModel> Books { get; set; }
Public DbSet<CategoryModel> Categories { get; set; }
}
```

8. Finally we will add an `Initializer` class, named `BooksInitializer.cs`, with the following content:

```
public class BooksInitializer :DropCreateDatabaseIfModelChanges<Bo
oksContext>
{
protected override void Seed(BooksContext context)
    {
    SeedCategories().ForEach(bc =>context.Categories.Add(bc));
    SeedBooks().ForEach(b =>context.Books.Add(b));
    }

private List<CategoryModel> SeedCategories()
    {
        List<CategoryModel> BookCategories = new
    List<CategoryModel>() {
        NewCategoryModel(){
                Id=1,
                Title = "Thriller"
            },
New CategoryModel(){
                Id=2,
                Title = "Mystery"
            },
New CategoryModel(){
                Id=3,
                Title = "Sci-fi"
            },
New CategoryModel(){
                Id=4,
                Title = "Computer Science"
            }
        };
```

```
Return BookCategories;
    }

    private List<BookModel>SeedBooks()
    {
        List<BookModel> Books = new List<BookModel>() {
        new BookModel(){
                    Id=1,
                    Title = ".NET 4.5 First Look",
CategoryId = 4,
                    Description = "A book to quickly and
practically get into .NET 4.5"
            },
        New BookModel(){
                    Id=2,
                    Title = "The lost book of Agatha Christie",
        CategoryId=1
                }
            };
        return Books;
        }


    }
```

9. We will open the `Global.asax` code behind the file and add the following line of code in the `Application_Start` method (note that we will need to add two `usings` clauses, one for `System.Data.Entity` file and another to access the Code First files):

```
Database.SetInitializer<BooksContext>(new BooksInitializer());
```

10. Open the `Web.config` file and comment the `DefaultConnection` connection string and add a connection string that will create the database in the `App_Data` folder. The new connection string is the following:

```
<add name="BooksContext"providerName="System.Data.SqlClient"
connectionString="Data Source=(LocalDB)\v11.0;AttachDbFilename=|Da
taDirectory|\wfSampleApp.mdf;Integrated Security=True"/>
```

11. Next we will add a new item of type **Web Form using Master Page** and name it `Books.aspx`.

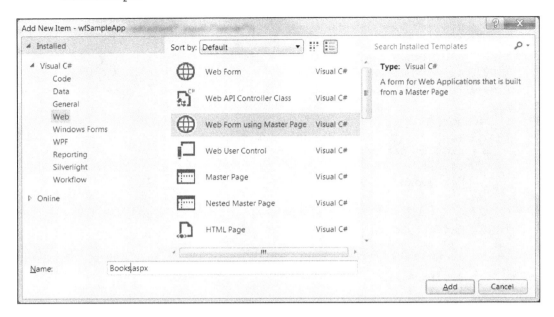

12. On pressing the **Add** button, the following dialogue will appear, where we will select the default master page and click on **OK**:

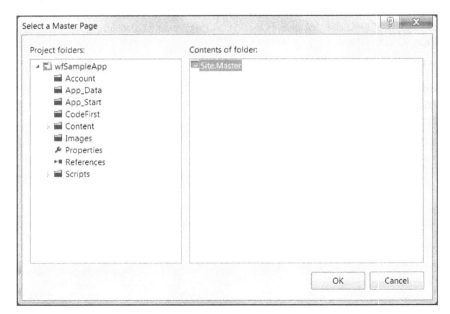

13. Add another item of the same type, with the name `Book.aspx`.

14. We will open the `Site.Master` page, look for the `<nav>`element in the header section, and change it to match the following code:

```
<nav>
<ul id="menu">
<li><a runat="server" href="~/">Home</a></li>
<li><a id="A1" runat="server" href="~/Books.aspx">Books</a></li>
<li><a runat="server" href="~/About.aspx">About</a></li>
<li><a runat="server" href="~/Contact.aspx">Contact</a></li>
</ul>
</nav>
```

15. Now open the `Site.Master` page code and type the method that we will use to provide the information to our interface so that it can be rendered. Create a function with the name `GetBooksCategories` with the following content:

```
public IQueryable<CategoryModel> GetBookCategories()
{
BooksContext dbBooks = new BooksContext();
DbSet<CategoryModel> dbSetCategories = dbBooks.Categories;

return (dbSetCategories as IQueryable<CategoryModel>);
}
```

16. We will update our UI to provide a visual for this data, by opening the `Site.Master` page and locating the `<div id="body">` section. Insert the following code just under that:

```
<section style="text-align: center; background-color: #fff">
<asp:ListView
ID="ListBookCategories"
ItemType="wfSampleApp.CodeFirst.CategoryModel"
runat="server"
SelectMethod="GetBookCategories">
<ItemTemplate>
<a href="Books.aspx?id=<%#: Item.Id %>"><%#: Item.Title %></a>
</ItemTemplate>
<ItemSeparatorTemplate> | </ItemSeparatorTemplate>
</asp:ListView>
</section>
```

17. If we have named our project differently, we should be aware of the name changes and correct it on the `ItemType` attribute in the previous code.

18. It would be interesting to go to `Item.Id` line of code and delete the **Id** text. This can be easily accomplished with the following tip: place the cursor in front of the **.** and press *Ctrl* + the Space bar to call intelli-sense to our aid. We should see the intelli-sense's help popup as shown in the following screenshot:

```
            runat="server"
            SelectMethod="GetBookCategories">
            <ItemTemplate>
                <a href="Books.aspx?id=<%#: Item. %>"><%#: Item.Title %></a>
            </ItemTemplate>                          Books
            <ItemSeparatorTemplate>| </ItemSepara   Description
        </asp:ListView>                              Equals
    </section>                                       GetHashCode
                                                     GetType
    <asp:ContentPlaceHolder runat="server" ID="Fe   Id          int CategoryModel.Id
    <section class="content-wrapper main-content     Title
        <asp:ContentPlaceHolder runat="server" ID   ToString          '>
```

19. We should execute the application, which will result in the database being created and the main page rendering as illustrated in the following image.

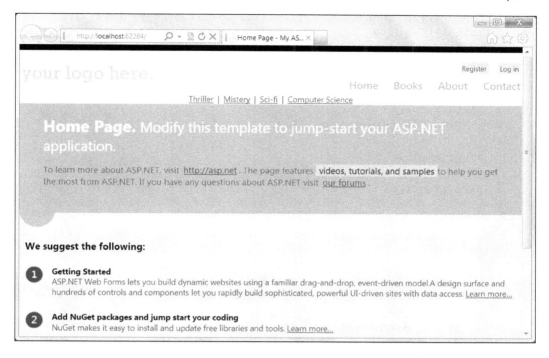

20. Open the `Books.aspx` file and add `ListViewcontrol` code in the **Featured Content** section.

21. Add the following code to it:

```
<asp:ListView
ID="BooksList"
runat="server"
DataKeyNames="Id"
ItemType="wfSampleApp.CodeFirst.BookModel"
SelectMethod="Books_GetData"
>

<EmptyDataTemplate>
<asp:Label ID="EmptyBooksLabel" runat="server" Text="We found no
books..."></asp:Label>
</EmptyDataTemplate>

<ItemTemplate>
<br />
```

```
<b>Book :</b><a href="Book.aspx?Id=<%#: Item.Id %>"><%#: Item.
Title %></a>
<br />
<b>On sale: </b>
<asp:CheckBox
ID="CheckBox1"
runat="server"
Checked='<%# Item.IsOnSale %>'
          />
</ItemTemplate>

</asp:ListView>
```

22. In the `Books.aspx.cs` code, add the following method:

```
Public IQueryable<BookModel> Books_GetData([QueryString("Id")]
int? Id)
{
    BooksContext dbBooks = new BooksContext();
    IQueryable<BookModel> dbSetBooks = dbBooks.Books;

    if (Id.HasValue&& Id > 0)
    {
        dbSetBooks = from b in dbSetBooks
        where b.CategoryId == Id
        select b;
    }

Return dbSetBooks;
}
```

23. Note that we need to add the following `Using` statements:

```
Using System.Web.ModelBinding;
Using wfSampleApp.CodeFirst;
```

24. If we execute the application now, when we click on the top category, we should navigate to the `Books.aspx`, passing the parameter of category ID. This should show the books of that category; if there are none, the **We found no books...** message should be shown.

25. Next we will open the `Book.aspx` file and its code.

26. In the `Book.aspx` file, we will add the following code in the **Featured Content** section:

```
<asp:FormView
ID="BookDetails"
runat="server"
DataKeyNames="Id"
ItemType="wfSampleApp.CodeFirst.BookModel"
SelectMethod="BookDetails_GetItem"
>
<ItemTemplate>
<h1><%#: Item.Title %></h1><br />
<b>Description:</b><br />
<%#: Item.Description %><br />
<b>On Sale:</b><asp:CheckBox ID="CheckBox1" runat="server"
Checked='<%# Item.IsOnSale %>' /><br />
<b>Rating:</b><%#: Item.BookRating %><br />
</ItemTemplate>
</asp:FormView>
```

27. In the code behind the file, we will add the following `select` method. We can automatically create its signature after entering the `select` method property on the `FormView` control. Visual Studio's intelli-sense will ask us if we want to create the method. The code is as follows:

```
Public BookModel BookDetails_GetItem([QueryString("Id")] int? Id)
{
BooksContext dbBooks = new BooksContext();
IQueryable<BookModel> dbSetBooks = dbBooks.Books;

if (Id.HasValue && Id > 0)
    {
    dbSetBooks = from b in dbSetBooks
    where b.Id == Id
    select b;
    }

Return dbSetBooks.First();
}
```

28. Finally we will select `Books.aspx` as the default page and execute the application. Upon execution, we should see the `Books.aspx` page inside the `Site.Master` page, displaying all the books since we are not applying any filter by default:

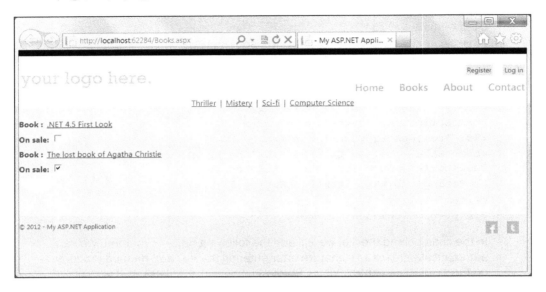

29. If we click on the **Computer Science** link at the top, we will be filtering by book category and displaying only the books from this category.

30. Next we will click on a book link, located on its name, and we should see the `Book.aspx` page showing the details of that book, as shown in the following screenshot:

How it works...

We created an ASP.NET Web Form using some of the new capabilities of ASP.NET 4.5.

We started by creating the CodeFirst model through Entity Framework, which we added through NuGet. Note that the previous chapter is dedicated to Entity Framework and is recommended to be read before the current one. We manually added the models for the book and for the categories of books. Next we created a `BooksContext` class that inherits from `DbContext` and an `Initializer` class that we will use to seed the database with initial data when it is created. Note that we use `DropCreateDatabaseIfModelChanges<Books Context>`, which means this will be executed only when there is any change in the database.

We have also used some data annotations attributes on our model classes, which will directly affect the database and the user input validation. An example of this is the `[Required]` attribute, which adds the input validation rule that this property must not be null.

The `DbContext` base class we used is from the Entity Framework and handles most of the CodeFirst database creation and updates magic transparently for us.

The `DropCreateDatabaseIfModelChanges` base class provides a default implementation of a class to handle the creation phase of a database, which we will use for the seed method mainly.

Following that, we set up a connection string with the database context with `BooksContext` as the class name, so we will create a database file for this data context, in the `App_Data` folder.

In the `Global.asax` code in the `Application_Start` method, we define an instance of this class as the database initializer for `BooksContext` with `Database.SetInitializer< BooksContext>(new booksInitializer())`. This class will be executed every time the database is created and provides two methods that we can override, `InitializeDatabase` and `Seed`.

Next we set up the UI, creating two pages: `Books.aspx` and `book.aspx`. On the `Site. Master` page, we added a link to the `Books.aspx` page to its navigation menu, identified by the `<nav>` tag. `<nav>` is an HTML5 element, supported with full intelli-sense in Visual Studio 2012, among other languages.

We added a custom method to return the categories on the `Site.Master` page code, which gets an instance of `BooksContext` class and collects the list of the database categories into `DbSet`. They are then returned as `IQueryable` database categories so that the UI is able to consume them properly.

In order to use this, we are adding a `ListView` control into the body of the `Site.Master` page using model binding. The use of the proper item type enforces type validation in our strongly typed models, and we can rely on intelli-sense for help on properties, methods, and so on. We choose our previously defined `GetBookCategories` method as a select method, located in our `Site.Master` code.

If we take a look at the ASP.NET code containing the `<%#: Item.Id%>` data-binding expression, the `:` after the `#` indicates that the resulting expression must be HTML-encoded, which is good for avoiding HTML and XSS (Cross Site Scripting) attacks. The item expression determines the bound property from our bound object. We also checked that this item has full intelli-sense support for the data model/type it is bound to.

When we execute the application for the first time and create a `DataContext` instance, the database is created—that is, if it didn't exist previously.

Continuing with application development, we added the functionality for the Books and the Books pages, using the new model binding to bind the data to our UI elements. The only thing we need to do is to define the `Select` method to get the data, which is done automatically (well, we do have to associate the method with the UI but that's all it takes).

On the Books and Book pages, in the code behind the `Select` methods, we have used the `QueryStringAttribute` class to get the query string ID that we are passing from the `Categories` menu we built earlier. In fact, ASP.NET makes this really easy in the form of value providers that we can use directly for other usual sources such as query string parameters, cookies, and session state. This attribute is provided to us from the `System.Web.ModelBinding` namespace, as can be seen in the following screenshot:

```
public BookModel BookDetails_GetItem([QueryString("Id")] int? Id)
{
                                      class System.Web.ModelBinding.QueryStringAttribute
    BooksContext dbBooks = new BooksCo Represents an attribute that specifies that model binding values are provided by a query string value.
    IQueryable<BookModel> dbSetBooks =
```

With this, we have explored some of the new and most interesting features of ASP.NET 4.5, ending with a completely functional website.

There's more...

We now have a grasp of the power of ASP.NET Web Forms, with model binding, the use of strongly typed data controls, HTML5 support, improved intelli-sense support, and its integration with CodeFirst.

It would be interesting to explore the rest of the data controls provided by ASP.NET to familiarize ourselves with the showcased features (strongly typed data controls and model binding) and to implement double binding with the `BindItem` element for data-input scenarios.

Configuring our application to use unobtrusive validation

This new feature will allow us to configure our validator controls for the use of unobtrusive client validation logic in a very simple way. A very significant benefit of doing this is the reduction of the amount of JavaScript rendered in the page, making it substantially smaller.

Note that unobtrusive means not obtrusive or undesirably noticeable, which is generally a good practice for JavaScript, meaning that there is a separation of responsibility between the web page (presentation) and its behavior.

Getting ready

In order to use this recipe you should have Visual Studio 2012. We will use this as well as the application generated from our previous recipe.

How to do it...

Here we will create a sample app and see how to apply unobtrusive validation to it and how it affects the resulting HTML.

1. Open our previous ASP.NET application or create a new one.
2. Open the `Web.Config` file.
3. Locate the `<appSettings>` element.
4. If it doesn't exist, add the following setting inside the element found previously:

   ```
   <add key="ValidationSettings:UnobtrusiveValidationMode"
   value="none" />
   ```

5. We will open our `Book.aspx` page and add the following code (a control and two validators) at the end of the `ItemTemplate` section:

```
<asp:TextBoxID="TbValidation"runat="server"/>
<asp:RequiredFieldValidatorID="tbvalidator1"runat="server"ErrorMes
sage="The field is required.."
ControlToValidate="TbValidation"EnableClientScript="true"/>
<asp:RangeValidatorID="tbrangevalidator1"runat="server"ErrorMessag
e="The range allowed is from 10 to 100"
ControlToValidate="TbValidation"EnableClientScript="true"/>
```

6. Next we execute the application and will see that the generated HTML looks as follows:

```
<input name="ctl00$FeaturedContent$BookDetails$TbValidation"
type="text" id="FeaturedContent_BookDetails_TbValidation" />
<span id="FeaturedContent_BookDetails_tbvalidator1"
style="visibility:hidden;">The field is required..</span>
<span id="FeaturedContent_BookDetails_tbrangevalidator1"
style="visibility:hidden;">The range allowed is from 10 to 100</
span>
```

7. We can see that the handling of this validations has generated a lot of JavaScript code after the HTML code:

```
<script type="text/javascript">
//<![CDATA[
var Page_Validators =  new Array(document.
getElementById("FeaturedContent_BookDetails_tbvalidator1"),
document.getElementById("FeaturedContent_BookDetails_
tbrangevalidator1"));
//]]>
</script>

<script type="text/javascript">
//<![CDATA[
var FeaturedContent_BookDetails_tbvalidator1 = document.all
? document.all["FeaturedContent_BookDetails_tbvalidator1"]
: document.getElementById("FeaturedContent_BookDetails_
tbvalidator1");
FeaturedContent_BookDetails_tbvalidator1.controltovalidate =
"FeaturedContent_BookDetails_TbValidation";
FeaturedContent_BookDetails_tbvalidator1.errormessage = "The field
is required..";
FeaturedContent_BookDetails_tbvalidator1.evaluationfunction =
"RequiredFieldValidatorEvaluateIsValid";
FeaturedContent_BookDetails_tbvalidator1.initialvalue = "";
```

```
var FeaturedContent_BookDetails_tbrangevalidator1 = document.all
? document.all["FeaturedContent_BookDetails_tbrangevalidator1"]
: document.getElementById("FeaturedContent_BookDetails_
tbrangevalidator1");
FeaturedContent_BookDetails_tbrangevalidator1.controltovalidate =
"FeaturedContent_BookDetails_TbValidation";
FeaturedContent_BookDetails_tbrangevalidator1.errormessage = "The
range allowed is from 10 to 100";
FeaturedContent_BookDetails_tbrangevalidator1.evaluationfunction =
"RangeValidatorEvaluateIsValid";
FeaturedContent_BookDetails_tbrangevalidator1.maximumvalue = "";
FeaturedContent_BookDetails_tbrangevalidator1.minimumvalue = "";
//]]>
</script>


<script type="text/javascript">
//<![CDATA[

var Page_ValidationActive = false;
if (typeof(ValidatorOnLoad) == "function") {
    ValidatorOnLoad();
}

function ValidatorOnSubmit() {
    if (Page_ValidationActive) {
        return ValidatorCommonOnSubmit();
    }
    else {
        return true;
    }
}

document.getElementById('FeaturedContent_BookDetails_
tbvalidator1').dispose = function() {
    Array.remove(Page_Validators, document.
getElementById('FeaturedContent_BookDetails_tbvalidator1'));
}

document.getElementById('FeaturedContent_BookDetails_
tbrangevalidator1').dispose = function() {
```

```
        Array.remove(Page_Validators, document.
getElementById('FeaturedContent_BookDetails_tbrangevalidator1'));
    }
//]]>
</script>
```

8. We will go back to the settings in the `Web.config` file and change the value to `WebForms`:

```
<add key="ValidationSettings:UnobtrusiveValidationMode"
value="WebForms"    />
```

9. Executing the application again will generate the following code:

```
<input name="ctl00$FeaturedContent$BookDetails$TbValidation"
type="text" id="FeaturedContent_BookDetails_TbValidation" />
<span data-val-controltovalidate="FeaturedContent_
BookDetails_TbValidation" data-val-errormessage="The&#32;fi
eld&#32;is&#32;required.." id="FeaturedContent_BookDetails_
tbvalidator1" data-val="true" data-val-evaluationfunction="Re
quiredFieldValidatorEvaluateIsValid" data-val-initialvalue=""
style="visibility:hidden;">The field is required..</span>
<span data-val-controltovalidate="FeaturedContent_BookDetails_
TbValidation" data-val-errormessage="The&#32;range&#32;allowe
d&#32;is&#32;from&#32;10&#32;to&#32;100" id="FeaturedContent_
BookDetails_tbrangevalidator1" data-val="true" data-val-evaluatio
nfunction="RangeValidatorEvaluateIsValid" data-val-maximumvalue=""
data-val-minimumvalue="" style="visibility:hidden;">The range
allowed is from 10 to 100</span>
```

10. We can observe that this is different from before, with a few data attributes rendered that have the information the validator needs. On the other hand, we will find that no inline JavaScript code has been generated this time.

How it works...

We just had to add a setting into `Web.Config` file; however, unobtrusive validation is enabled by default in new projects, so in most cases, even if this setting is not there, it is active.

There's more...

We could also configure it from code, setting `System.UI.ValidationSettings.UnobtrusiveValidationMode` to `UnobtrusiveValidationMode.WebForms` or setting this on a particular page and changing the page's `UnobtrusiveValidationMode` property to `UnobtrusiveValidationMode.WebForms` or none.

Using Smart Tasks in the HTML editor

The HTML editor provides improved support for some of the server controls that used to have dialogues and wizards for their configuration and setup. Usually we had to do this from the design view or move our mouse to the properties to launch these configuration wizards.

With ASP.NET 4.5, we have them at our fingertips in our source code view.

Getting ready

In order to use this recipe you should have Visual Studio 2012.

How to do it...

In this recipe we are going to see how to activate and use the Smart Tasks in the HTML editor.

1. Open our previous ASP.NET application or create a new one.
2. Open the `Site.Master` page.
3. Locate the `<asp:ListView>` server control that we added (or add a new one).
4. Place our text input cursor in the code, over the tag; click on it so that it is selected.
5. We should see an underline glyph at the beginning of the element and it should appear highlighted, showing that it has been selected, as shown in the following screenshot:

```
<asp:ListView
    ID="ListBookCategories"
    ItemType="wfSampleApp.CodeFirst.CategoryModel"
    runat="server"
    SelectMethod="GetBookCategories">
    <ItemTemplate>
        <a href="Books.aspx?id=<%#: Item.Id %>"><%#: Item.Title %></a>
    </ItemTemplate>
    <ItemSeparatorTemplate>| </ItemSeparatorTemplate>
</asp:ListView>
```

6. When we click over the glyph or put the mouse over the `<asp:` tag, we will see that the smart task glyph expands into an arrow.

7. We can click on this arrow to expand the **Smart Tasks** panel or we can press *Ctrl + .* to directly expand it, as shown in the following screenshot.

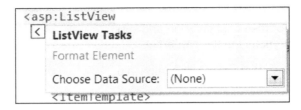

8. From there, we can select the data source selection, create a new one, and launch its wizard, as shown in the next screenshot:

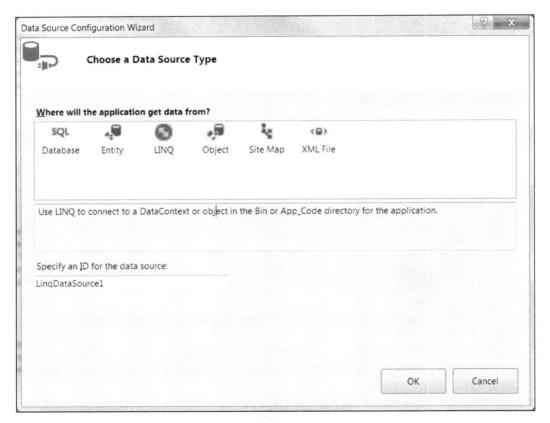

How it works...

We just saw how easy it is to use this time-saving new feature so that we do not have to leave our code panel to perform these tasks, improving our productivity, which always comes in handy.

Using WAI-ARIA support

Visual Studio 2012 fully supports the **Web Accessibility Initiative-Accessible Rich Internet Applications (WAI-ARIA)** standard, making it easier for us to create accessible websites. This is the Accessible Rich Internet Applications suite that provides a way to make web content and apps more accessible through this framework, and this in turn allows us to add attributes for identifying features regarding accessibility. Basically, ARIA is a set of semantic tags and attributes that identify features regarding accessibility in user interaction, how they relate to each other, and their state.

Getting ready

In order to use this recipe you should have Visual Studio 2012.

How to do it...

Here we will see how to use Visual Studio 2012's support for WAI-ARIA:

1. Open our previous ASP.NET Application or create a new one.
2. Open the `Site.Master` page.
3. Go to the `<nav>` element.
4. Press *Ctrl* + the Space bar.

5. We will be able to see all the WAI-ARIA attributes, which are prefixed with the **aria-** prefix, as we can see in the following screenshot:

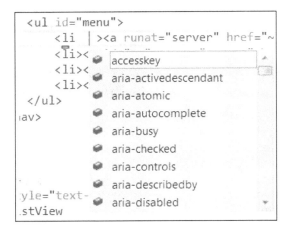

6. Now it is extremely easy to add the necessary semantics to our HTML5 document.

How it works...

It is really easy to add the WAI-ARIA attributes using the Visual Studio 2012 intelli-sense feature, which automatically recognizes them.

Using the Extract to User Control feature

Modularizing is always a good idea to simplify code. With the Extract to User Control feature, we have a powerful tool that will help us with this refactoring functionality.

Getting ready

In order to use this recipe you should have Visual Studio 2012.

How to do it...

Here we are going to show how to easily generate a user control from a section of code in our web page.

1. Open our previous ASP.NET application or create a new one.

2. If you created a new application, add a control and customize it to your liking.

3. Open the `Site.Master` page.

4. Go to the `div` body and select the `<section>` element surrounding it.

5. Right-click on the selected code and click on the **Extract to User Control** option.

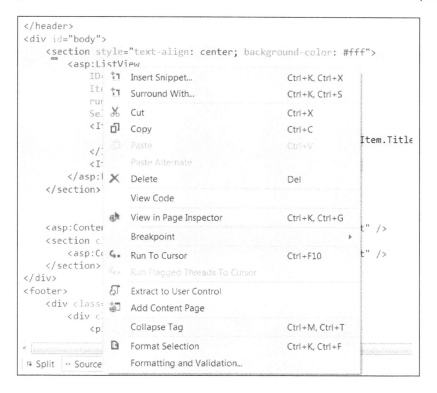

6. On the **Save as** dialog, assign the name `ListOfCategories.ascx` and click on the **OK** button.

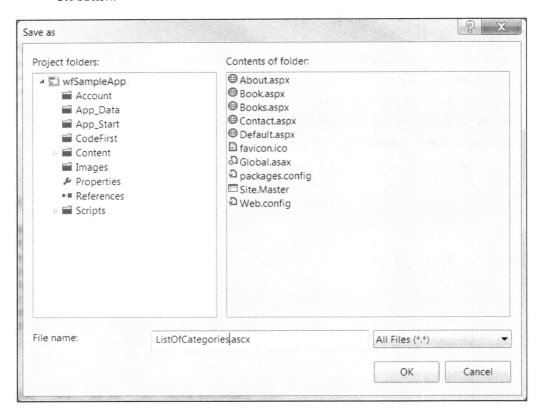

7. Now we will need to move the `GetBookCategories()` method from the code, as the related methods are not moved.

How it works...

We simply created a user control based on a section of our HTML code. We just have to remember to move the methods and code that are not moved.

Using the Page Inspector feature

Page Inspector is a tool that renders our pages in our Visual Studio 2012 IDE and lets us examine the source code and its output. It is great to determine which piece of code has produced a specific HTML markup code.

Getting ready

In order to use this recipe you should have Visual Studio 2012.

How to do it...

In this section we are going to see how to use the Page Inspector to inspect a page along with its styles.

1. Open our previous ASP.NET application.

2. Right-click on the `Books.aspx` page and select the **View in Page Inspector** option.

3. Once the **Page Inspector** panel opens, click on the **Inspect** button at the bottom of the rendered page and click on the **Categories** selector. The bottom section should showcase the rendered HTML; we should see the applied styles on our left and the ASP.NET code that generates the selected element on our right.

How it works...

The page inspector is an outstanding feature to discover where a concrete style is being applied or what is provoking a change in our interface. It allows us to see the source HTML, the styles, and the final generated code as well as the final rendering, hence becoming a really useful tool.

Creating an asynchronous HTTP module

ASP.NET 4.5 provides us with the full C# language features described previously in *Chapter 2, Exploring the Top New Features of the CLR*. Also, the additional methods and features make it easier for us to work with asynchronous language features.

This helps enormously in writing asynchronous HTTP modules and handlers.

Performance is also improved, as the model is asynchronous; it doesn't keep the thread blocked until the request is completed.

Getting ready

In order to use this recipe you should have Visual Studio 2012.

How to do it...

We are going to create an asynchronous HTTP module. An HTTP module allows us to intercept HTTP requests for modifying those requests so we can generate a response in a customized way.

1. Create a new class library project and name it `AsyncHTTPModule`.
2. Add a reference to the `System.Web` assembly.
3. Add a class and name it `CustomModule`. Note that we could as well add an item of type `ASP.NET`, which would do most of the following for us:
    - Add a `Using` clause to the `System.Web` page
    - Make the class implement `IHttpModule`
    - Right-click on the interface and click on the **Implement interface** option
    - Add the following asynchronous method:

```
private async Task getWebPageContent(object caller, EventArgs e)
{
WebClient wc = new WebClient();
```

```
var result = await wc.DownloadStringTaskAsync
("http://www.packtpub.com/");

HttpApplication app = (HttpApplication)caller;
app.Response.Write(result);
}
```

4. Note that we will need to add a `Using` clause to `System.Net` to use the `WebClient` method.

5. Next we will implement the `Init` method:

```
public void Init(HttpApplication context)
{
    // We use the EventHandlerTaskAsyncHelper to wrap the task
    based method to use with the "old" async programming model.
    EventHandlerTaskAsyncHelper asyncHelper = new EventHandlerTaskAsyn
    cHelper(getWebPageContent);

    // The helper class instance generates the Begin/End methods
    for us from a Task Function.
    context.AddOnPostAuthorizeRequestAsync(asyncHelper.
    BeginEventHandler, asyncHelper.EndEventHandler);
}
```

6. We should now implement the `dispose` method. Leaving it empty will do for now.

7. And we have our ASP.NET 4.5 asynchronous module ready.

How it works...

In this scenario, the request thread is released when the request has been initiated and a new thread is created when the request finishes, with the response being received on a brand new thread.

Implementing an asynchronous HTTP module fits in perfectly with the core of this behavior.

We implemented `IHttpModule` and created an asynchronous task. This method can be awaited, which means that it will not block the thread on which it is executed; when it has finished, it will continue from the point where it was awaited, control being returned to the caller of the async method. When an async method or the task it returns finishes, it invokes its continuation from where it left off.

After defining the asynchronous method, which will download the `www.packtpub.com` website asynchronously and return it as the response, we need to assign it so it can be used by the HTTP module.

We do this with the `EventHandlerTaskAsyncHelper` class, which we get from the `System.Web` namespace.

This helper method is meant to integrate a task-based method with the programming model exposed by the ASP.NET HTTP pipeline, which will assign the `Begin` and `End` methods to the async helper's `BeginEventHandler` and `EndEventHandler` event handlers.

There's more...

It would be interesting to explore the asynchronous HTTP handler feature of ASP.NET 4.5 since the new async features would allow us to significantly improve the performance of our applications.

6
Implementing WPF's new features

In this chapter we will cover:

- ▸ Implementing asynchronous error handling with `INotifyDataErrorInfo`
- ▸ Using the `WeakEvent` pattern with `WeakEventManager`
- ▸ Using the dispatcher's new features
- ▸ Data binding to static properties
- ▸ Throttling the data source update delays
- ▸ LiveShaping — repositioning elements when bound data changes

Introduction

WPF has been enhanced in .NET 4.5, including new and improved controls, such as the ribbon, better data validation, and the `INotifyDataErrorInfo` interface, to get into the world of asynchronous data validation. The main new features of .NET 4.5 are as follows:

- ▸ Improved performance for displaying large sets of data.
- ▸ Improvements in data binding, which involves binding to static properties, custom types (`ICustomTypeProvider`), reacting when the data context is disconnected, and introducing timeouts for property changes. We can also obtain the data binding information for a binding expression.
- ▸ Data source update delays help us configure a delay to update a data source from the UI, which can be very useful to improve our application's performance.

- Better weak-event pattern support, now accepting markup extensions.
- LiveShaping or repositioning of data as the values change.
- Accessing collections on the UI threads.

In the following sections, we will cover and explain some of the most relevant changes, improvements, and actions.

Implementing asynchronous error handling with INotifyDataErrorInfo

The INotifyDataErrorInfo interface has been a .NET citizen for some time, at least for Silverlight developers. It brought a new improved system for validating data, which we now have in WPF, with all of its power and interesting things to discover.

Getting ready

In order to use this recipe you should have Visual Studio 2012 installed.

How to do it...

In this recipe we will explain how to use this new powerful feature of WPF in .NET 4.5.

1. First, open Visual Studio 2012 and create a new project. We will select the **WPF Application** template from the **Visual C#** category and name it WPFValidation.

2. Create a class named BaseClass.cs. Edit it and implement the interfaces INotifyPropertyChanged and IDataErrorInfo. We can copy the following code inside it:

```
public abstract class BaseClass : INotifyPropertyChanged,
INotifyDataErrorInfo
{
    private static Dictionary<string, PropertyChangedEventArgs>
argumentInstances = new Dictionary<string,
PropertyChangedEventArgs>();
    private Dictionary<string, List<string>> errors = new
Dictionary<string, List<string>>();

    public event PropertyChangedEventHandler PropertyChanged;
    public event EventHandler<DataErrorsChangedEventArgs>
ErrorsChanged;
```

```csharp
public bool HasErrors
{
    get { return this.errors.Count > 0; }
}

public IEnumerable GetErrors(string propertyName)
{
    if (string.IsNullOrEmpty(propertyName) ||
        !this.errors.ContainsKey(propertyName))
        return null;

    return this.errors[propertyName];
}

public void AddError(string propertyName, string error, bool
isWarning)
{
    if (!this.errors.ContainsKey(propertyName))
        this.errors[propertyName] = new List<string>();

    if (!this.errors[propertyName].Contains(error))
    {
        if (isWarning)
            this.errors[propertyName].Add(error);
        else
            this.errors[propertyName].Insert(0, error);
    }

    this.RaiseErrorsChanged(propertyName);
}

public void RemoveError(string propertyName, string error)
{
    if (this.errors.ContainsKey(propertyName) &&
        this.errors[propertyName].Contains(error))
    {
        this.errors[propertyName].Remove(error);

        if (this.errors[propertyName].Count == 0)
            this.errors.Remove(propertyName);
    }
```

```
            this.RaiseErrorsChanged(propertyName);
        }

        public void RaiseErrorsChanged(string propertyName)
        {
            if (this.ErrorsChanged != null)
                this.ErrorsChanged(this, new DataErrorsChangedEventArg
    s(propertyName));
        }

        protected virtual void OnPropertyChanged(string propertyName)
        {
            if (this.PropertyChanged != null)
                this.PropertyChanged(this, new PropertyChangedEventArg
    s(propertyName));
        }
    }
```

3. We can now add a class that inherits this `BaseClass`, so let's add the `BooksModel` class to the equation:

```
class BooksModel : BaseClass
{
    private string name;
    public string Name
    {
        get { return name; }
        set
        {
            name = value;
            if ((name.Length < 2) || (name.Length > 150)) {
                    this.AddError("Name", "The name must be over 2
    characters and less than 150 characters", false);
            }
            OnPropertyChanged("Name");
        }
    }

    private String isbn;
    public String ISBN
    {
        get { return isbn; }
        set {
```

```
            isbn = value;
            ValidateISBN();
        }
    }

    private async Task ValidateISBN()
    {
        await Wait_a_bit();

        Random rnd = new Random(DateTime.Now.Millisecond);
        int likeness = rnd.Next(0, 6);
        if (likeness > 2)
        {
            this.AddError("ISBN", "I don't like the ISBN", false);
        }
        else
        {
            this.RemoveError("ISBN", "I don't like the ISBN");
        }
    }

    private Task Wait_a_bit() {
        return Task.Run(() => Thread.Sleep(1500));
    }
}
```

4. Continuing, we will open and edit the `MainWindow.xaml` file to provide a user interface, as follows:

```xml
<Window x:Class="INotifyDataErrorInfoWPF.MainWindow"
        xmlns="http://schemas.microsoft.com/winfx/2006/xaml/
presentation"
        xmlns:x="http://schemas.microsoft.com/winfx/2006/xaml"
        Title="MainWindow" Height="150" Width="425">
    <Grid Margin="0,0,0.4,-0.4">
        <Grid.ColumnDefinitions>
            <ColumnDefinition Width="12.8"/>
            <ColumnDefinition Width="65*"/>
            <ColumnDefinition/>
        </Grid.ColumnDefinitions>
        <Grid.RowDefinitions>
            <RowDefinition Height="15.2"/>
            <RowDefinition/>
```

```
            </Grid.RowDefinitions>
            <Grid Margin="0.2,15,8.2,0.4" Grid.Column="1" Grid.
RowSpan="2">
                <Grid.ColumnDefinitions>
                    <ColumnDefinition Width="7*"/>
                    <ColumnDefinition Width="23*"/>
                </Grid.ColumnDefinitions>
                <Grid.RowDefinitions>
                    <RowDefinition Height="32"/>
                    <RowDefinition Height="32"/>
                    <RowDefinition/>
                    <RowDefinition Height="4*"/>
                </Grid.RowDefinitions>
                <Label Content="Name:"/>
                <Label Content="ISBN:" Grid.Row="1"/>
                <TextBox x:Name="tbName"
            Text="{Binding Name, Mode=TwoWay, ValidatesOnNotifyDataErr
ors=True}"
            Grid.Column="1"
            Margin="2,2,2.4,2"
                        />
                <TextBox x:Name="tbISBN"
            Text="{Binding ISBN, Mode=TwoWay, ValidatesOnNotifyDataErr
ors=True}"
            Grid.Column="1" Grid.Row="1"
            Margin="2,2,1.4,2"
                        />
            </Grid>
        </Grid>
</Window>
```

5. Next, we will add some code in it to create an instance of `BooksModel` and set it as the context of the view. We will edit the `MainWindow` constructor as follows:

```
public MainWindow()
{
    InitializeComponent();

    BooksModel bm = new BooksModel();
    this.DataContext = bm;
}
```

6. If we run our application and introduce some information, for example, if we type a character in the **Name** field and exit it, we should see the input field surrounded by a red line, as shown in the following screenshot:

Additionally, if we input some text in the **ISBN** field, it gets *validated* (in a bit more than a second) by a random function that decides whether it likes the value or not. So we can see an asynchronous validation in place. Note that the asynchronous nature of this validation would allow us to make it happen on the server, which could have more advanced business validation rules, that make sense to delegate some business validation to it.

How it works...

If we take a look at the INotifyDataErrorInfo class diagram in the following screenshot, we can appreciate its simplicity. Its interface exposes an **ErrorsChanged** event that is fired whenever an error is detected or removed, a **HasErrors** read-only property, and a **GetErrors** method that returns IEnumerable with the error list associated with the requested property:

We implemented these elements on BaseClass, together with the usual event for INotifyPropertyChanged.

Additionally, we created the `AddError` and `RemoveError` helper methods to handle the addition and removal of errors in an easy way. Errors are automatically broadcasted to anybody who is listening to them—mainly the bindings in place.

The `RaiseErrorsChanged` method will raise the event to notify that the errors have changed, which will happen whenever we have added or removed an error.

Next, we have implemented the `BookModel` class, which inherits from `BaseClass`. For both its properties, we set up validations on its property setters.

For the first property, `Name`, we just check that its length is between 2 and 150 and if it is not we call the `AddError` method with the name of the property and the error. Note that there is a third parameter, which indicates if this is a warning.

For the `ISBN` property, we perform an asynchronous validation using the `async` method `ValidateISBN()`. As an example, it will first await an `async` method, named `Wait_a_bit()`, that just sleeps for 1.5 seconds, and then decides randomly whether the value is valid or not.

This example showcases that we could in fact go to the server, ask for it to validate the value, see if the updated ISBN already exists or is registered, and if it does, return an error.

Finally, we have created a very simple interface to enter data into two `TextBox` controls, which we have bound to the properties. Remember we need to add `ValidatesOnNotifyDataErrors = True`. If we don't do this, the UI field will not react to the validation events.

There's more...

This event based validation system is in many ways similar to `INotifyPropertyInfo` and is ideal for asynchronous validation systems that can be run on the server. Additionally, this enables us to implement really advanced scenarios such as:

- ► Performing cross-property validations that apply to more than one field, for example, the typical *from – to* range of dates. Now, we can mark both as invalid when the *from* date is greater than the *to* date.
- ► Hierarchical validation systems are those in which an error in a property element is cascaded to its parent, so if a piece of the complete hierarchy is invalid, the whole structure of data is invalidated.

Using the WeakEvent pattern with WeakEventManager

Normal event handlers are defined using the += operator and the source keeps a reference to its listeners. If this reference is not removed, it prevents the listener from receiving garbage data. This is one of the most common causes of memory leaks, which are now much easier to avoid.

WPF 4.5 WeakEventManager provides us with a central event dispatching capability that allows the listeners to be de-allocated from memory, while the event is still alive.

While this is not a strictly new behavior, WPF 4.5 brings us enhanced support to set up a weak reference to an event. Prior to this version of WPF, we had to create a weak event manager for every event. This is not the case anymore. Now we can use a generic WeakEventManager for this; let's see how it works.

Getting ready

In order to use this recipe you should have Visual Studio 2012 installed.

How to do it...

Here we will implement some events with the WeakEventManager class.

1. First, open Visual Studio 2012 and create a new project. We will select the **WPF Application** template from the **Visual C#** category and name it WPFWeakEvents.

2. Open the MainWindow.xaml view and add a **Button Click** event, name it btnRaiseEvent, and put Raise an event... in the content.

3. Open the MainWindow.xaml.cs code and change the MainWindow class code to this:

```
public partial class MainWindow : Window
{
    public MainWindow()
    {
        InitializeComponent();

        // The leaking way
        // this.btnRaiseEvent.Click += btnRaiseEvent_Click;

        SetupWeakEventManager();
    }
}
```

```
void btnRaiseEvent_Click(object sender, RoutedEventArgs e)
{
    MessageBox.Show("Hey, use the WeakEventManager or I might
leak...");
}

private void SetupWeakEventManager()
{
    WeakEventManager<Button, RoutedEventArgs>.AddHandler(this.
btnRaiseEvent, "Click", btnRaiseEvent_Click);
}
}
```

4. And that's it! We just implemented the WeakEventManager class to handle the **Button Click** event in a proper way that will provide a safer event handling, which will not provoke memory leaks.

How it works...

We used the WeakEventManager class, which provides us with a way to add and remove a handler through static methods, so we now have a much easier way to add *weak* event handlers.

Take a look at the WeakEventManager generic class, pictured in the following screenshot:

To use the WeakEventManager class, we only need to provide the type that raises the event and the type with the event's data. Next, we invoke the AddHandler method, which requires the specific object that we are subscribing to, the event name, and the associated event handler.

We should also use the `RemoveHandler` method to remove the event handler, which is a *polite* behavior for our code, wherever possible.

Before this WPF version, we had to implement the `IWeakEventListener` interface on the event listeners, which is no longer required. However, it can still be useful in some scenarios—bear in mind that this is driven by reflection and thus has a performance penalty. This could be interesting for implementing a custom control or a library, avoiding performance penalties. Also doing so could be interesting for testing purposes.

Using the dispatcher's new features

The `Dispatcher` class is a very common way of accessing the UI thread while we are on another thread.

With WPF 4.5 we have some new methods for synchronous and asynchronous operations, which make this `Dispatcher` class more *async and await friendly*. Another improvement is that `Dispatcher.Invoke` and `Dispatcher.InvokeAsync` are now able to return a value.

Finally, we also have a new parameter of `CancellationToken` type, which provides the obvious capability of being able to cancel dispatched tasks.

Getting ready

In order to use this recipe you should have Visual Studio 2012 installed.

How to do it...

In the following steps we will see how to use the `Dispatcher` class to dispatch a task that accesses the UI thread.

1. First open Visual Studio 2012 and create a new project. We will select the **WPF Application** template from the **Visual C#** category and name it `WPFDispatcher`.

2. Open the `MainWindow.xaml` view and add a **Button Click** event, name it `btnDispatcher` and enter 1 as the content.

3. Open the `MainWindow.xaml.cs` code and change the `MainWindow` class code as follows:

```
public MainWindow()
{
    InitializeComponent();
```

```
            this.btnDispatcher.Click += btnDispatcher_Click;
    }


    void btnDispatcher_Click(object sender, RoutedEventArgs e)
    {
        TestNewDispatcherAsyncMethod();
    }


    public async void TestNewDispatcherAsyncMethod() {
        // Usage of the InvokeAsync method
        var TaskDoSomething = await Dispatcher.InvokeAsync<Task<string
>>(DoSomething);

        // We wait for the task to finish
        TaskDoSomething.Wait();

        // Getting the result from the finished task
        string resultFromTask = TaskDoSomething.Result;

        // Usage of the Invoke method which returns a value of a
    defined type
        var returnedObject = Dispatcher.Invoke<string>(
    DoSomethingElse);
    }


    private string DoSomethingElse()
    {
        return "hi";
    }


    private async Task<string> DoSomething()
    {
        //As we are being dispatched we could access the UI thread and
    update-change something there...
        String num = this.btnDispatcher.Content.ToString();
        int iNum;
        int.TryParse(num, out iNum);
        iNum = iNum + 1;
        this.btnDispatcher.Content = iNum.ToString();
```

```
        return "I should do something...";
    }
```

4. We can now execute the code and click the button. For every click it will increase its value by one.

How it works...

We have used one of the new `Dispatcher` methods, which can be called asynchronously.

```
// Usage of the InvokeAsync method
var TaskDoSomething = await Dispatcher.InvokeAsync<Task<string>>(DoSo
mething);
```

The example illustrates how to receive the result of `Task` where we are changing a UI element and returning a value.

We can observe that we are executing a dispatcher operation asynchronously, which is in sync with the UI thread.

We are also invoking it in the *usual* non-asynchronous way with:

```
// Usage of the Invoke method which returns a value of a defined type
var returnedOject = Dispatcher.Invoke<string>( DoSomethingElse);
```

As you can see, we can now return a result value of a specific type with a `Dispatcher.Invoke` method.

To complete the example, the `DoSomething` asynchronous method makes a very simple change on the UI thread.

There's more...

If we take a look at the new methods that the `Dispatcher` class provides, we find the `CancellationToken` method, which enables us to cancel an action (or prevent it from being executed). This method belongs to the .NET 4.0 Cancellation Framework, which is useful for a proper implementation of the unit of work pattern.

We just saw how to use two of the most useful new methods, but there are a lot more to be explored.

Data binding to static properties

With WPF 4.5 we can now bind to static properties. Let's see how.

Getting ready

In order to use this recipe you should have Visual Studio 2012 installed.

How to do it...

In this recipe, we are going to see how to use the capability of WPF in .NET 4.5 to bind to static properties as well as how to define and notify their property changes.

1. First, open Visual Studio 2012 and create a new project. We will select the **WPF Application** template from the **Visual C#** category and name it WPFStaticPropertiesBinding.

2. Add a class and name it MyStaticDetails.cs, adding the following code:

```csharp
public class MyStaticDetails
{
    public static event EventHandler<PropertyChangedEventArgs>
StaticPropertyChanged;
    protected static void OnPropertyChanged(string propertyName)
    {
        if (StaticPropertyChanged != null)
            StaticPropertyChanged(null, new PropertyChangedEventAr
gs(propertyName));
    }


    private static int myAge;
    public static int MyAge
    {
        get { return myAge; }
        set {
            myAge = value;
            OnPropertyChanged("MyAge");
        }
    }

    private static string myName;
```

```
        public static string MyName
        {
            get { return myName; }
            set {
                myName = value;
                OnPropertyChanged("MyName");
            }
        }
    }
}
```

3. Open the `MainWindow.xaml.cs` code and change the `MainWindow` class code as follows:

```
public MainWindow()
{
    InitializeComponent();

    MyStaticDetails msd = new MyStaticDetails();
    MyStaticDetails.MyAge = 40;
    MyStaticDetails.MyName = "Jose Louis";

    this.DataContext = msd;
}
```

4. Open the `MainWindow.xaml` view and add two rows and two columns to the grid, then add two labels and two `TextBox` controls, and finally a binding expression to their **Text** property. The resulting XAML code should be similar to the following:

```
<Grid>
    <Grid.ColumnDefinitions>
        <ColumnDefinition Width="21*"/>
        <ColumnDefinition Width="64*"/>
    </Grid.ColumnDefinitions>
    <Grid.RowDefinitions>
        <RowDefinition Height="30"/>
        <RowDefinition Height="29.6"/>
        <RowDefinition/>
    </Grid.RowDefinitions>
    <Label Content="Name: " />
    <Label Content="Age: " Grid.Row="1"/>
    <TextBox Grid.Column="1" TextWrapping="Wrap"
             Text="{Binding MyName, Mode=TwoWay}"
             Margin="2"/>
```

```
<TextBox Grid.Column="1" Grid.Row="1" TextWrapping="Wrap"
         Text="{Binding MyAge, Mode=TwoWay}"
         Margin="2"/>
</Grid>
```

5. Add a breakpoint on the `MyName` setter.

6. Execute the application; we should see the following screen:

7. Go to the **Name** field and change it to `Pancho`, for example.

8. When we move the cursor out of the textbox (for example, by pressing the *Tab* key), we will see that the break point is properly hit so the binding works on both directions, as expected.

How it works...

We implemented one of the two static events that we have in .NET 4.5 to notify changes in static properties, specifically the `StaticPropertyChanged` event. We used it to pass a `PropertyChangedEventArgs` event to provide, in turn, the name of the property being changed. The implementation is very similar to that of our non-static `PropertyChanged` event.

```
public static event EventHandler<PropertyChangedEventArgs>
StaticPropertyChanged;
protected static void OnPropertyChanged(string propertyName)
{
    if (StaticPropertyChanged != null)
        StaticPropertyChanged(null, new PropertyChangedEventArgs(prop
ertyName));
}
```

As we already did with the `NotifyPropertyChanged` event, we now call the method we defined, to raise our `StaticPropertyChanged` event:

```
OnPropertyChanged("MyAge");
```

The rest of the implementation is the creation of an instance of `MyStaticDetails`, adding a default value and setting this as `DataContext` of the `MainWindow` UI.

On the `MainWindow` UI, we set up a grid with two rows and columns where we have placed the headings as labels and the controls to display and edit the data as textboxes.

Finally, we added a binding expression for the **Text** property for the textbox, using **TwoWay** binding in a standard fashion.

There's more...

We could have implemented the other interface:

```
public static event EventHandler MyPropertyChanged;
```

However, we would have needed to implement it for every property, since the events are named for each individual property name. In our case, we would have had the events, `MyAgeChanged` and `MyNameChanged`. This can be implemented for a reduced set of properties but is definitely not scalable.

Throttling data source update delays

With WPF 4.5, we can now control how the data source that is bound to a part of the UI, gets updated. The best example here is a slider bound to a value, which, for example, has to perform a calculation. With WPF 4.0, the property setter was called for every changed event that was launched by the binding in place and, if we didn't do anything to prevent the excessive calculations, we could end with a responsiveness problem. This could be even worse if some calculation was being performed in response, such as updating the total price.

Now, this doesn't happen, as we can control the delay after the property stops changing, before updating the source. This means that we can change a UI element and we can control how the bound property gets updated. Adding a delay to it will benefit our performance, so that thousands of updates cannot be thrown.

In the slider example, its `PropertyChanged` event was invoked many times for every movement. Now we can instruct it to get invoked a bit after the slider stops moving.

Getting ready

In order to use this recipe you should have Visual Studio 2012 installed.

How to do it...

Here we are going to see how to apply throttling properly to our bindings to make our application interface more responsive.

1. First, open Visual Studio 2012 and create a new project. We will select the **WPF Application** template from the **Visual C#** category and name it WPFAutoDelayedUpdates.

2. We will add the BaseClass.cs class from the *Implementing asynchronous error handling with INotifyDataErrorInfo* recipe, which implements the INotifyDataErrorInfo and the INotifyPropertyChanged interfaces for us.

3. Add a class and name it BookModel.cs, adding the following code:

```
class BookModel : BaseClass
{
    private int bookRating;

    public int BookRating
    {
        get { return bookRating; }
        set {
            ValidateRating();
            bookRating = value;
            OnPropertyChanged("BookRating");
        }
    }

    private async Task ValidateRating()
    {
        //await Wait_a_bit();
        Thread.Sleep(200);
        Random rnd = new Random(DateTime.Now.Millisecond);
        int likeness = rnd.Next(0, 6);
        if (likeness > 2)
        {
            this.AddError("BookRating", "The rating is not valid",
false);
        }
```

```
            else
            {
                this.RemoveError("BookRating", "The rating is not
valid");
            }
        }
    }
```

4. Go to the `MainWindow.xaml.cs` class and add the following code in the constructor:

```
public MainWindow()
{
    InitializeComponent();

    BookModel bm = new BookModel() {
        BookRating = 50
    };
    this.DataContext = bm;
}
```

5. Continuing, we will open the `MainWindow.xaml` class and create the interface. Divide the grid into two columns, one for the labels and another for the displayed and editable values. Add the `Slider` control for the editable values. The XAML code should look like the following:

```
<Window x:Class="WPFAutoDelayedUpdates.MainWindow"
        xmlns="http://schemas.microsoft.com/winfx/2006/xaml/
presentation"
        xmlns:x="http://schemas.microsoft.com/winfx/2006/xaml"
        Title="MainWindow" Height="350" Width="525">
    <Grid>
        <Grid.ColumnDefinitions>
            <ColumnDefinition Width="211*"/>
            <ColumnDefinition Width="299*"/>
        </Grid.ColumnDefinitions>
        <Grid.RowDefinitions>
            <RowDefinition Height="30"/>
            <RowDefinition Height="30"/>
            <RowDefinition Height="30"/>
            <RowDefinition Height="30"/>
            <RowDefinition/>
        </Grid.RowDefinitions>
        <Label Content="Select the book Rating" Grid.
ColumnSpan="2" Margin="0,0,0.4,0.4"/>
```

```
                <Label Content="Without Data Source Update Delay: "
        Margin="0,30,1.2,0.8" Grid.RowSpan="2"/>
                <Label Content="With Data Source Update Delay: " Grid.
        Row="2" Margin="0,0.2,1.2,0.2"/>
                <Label Content="The bound value: " Grid.Row="3" />
                <TextBox TextWrapping="Wrap" Text="{Binding BookRating,
        Mode=TwoWay}" Grid.Column="1" Grid.Row="3" IsReadOnly="True" />
                <Slider x:Name="SliderNotDelayed"
                        Value="{Binding BookRating, Mode=TwoWay}"
                        Grid.Column="1" Grid.Row="1" Margin="3"
        Maximum="100" />
                <Slider x:Name="SliderDelayed"
                        Value="{Binding BookRating, Mode=TwoWay,
        Delay=200}"
                        Grid.Column="1" Grid.Row="2" Margin="3"
        Maximum="100" />

            </Grid>
        </Window>
```

6. We will bind the `Sliders` and `TextBox` controls in TwoWay mode to the `BookRating` property. On the second binding, we specify the `Delay` keyword with a 200 milliseconds delay:

```
<Slider x:Name="SliderDelayed"
        Value="{Binding BookRating, Mode=TwoWay, Delay=200}"
        Grid.Column="1" Grid.Row="2" Margin="3" Maximum="100" />
```

7. When we execute the application we will see the following UI:

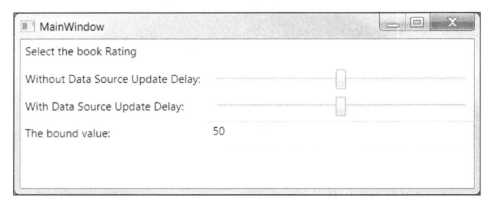

8. If we slide the first `Slider` to one side or the other, we will see that the response is sluggish, since the value is updated for every movement, invoking the setter, which executes a costly operation (`Thread.Sleep(200);`). The second `Slider` has a much smoother response, because it only raises the setter 200 milliseconds after its value has finished changing.

9. The power of this feature becomes crystal clear with this example. It will make life much easier for yourself and your users.

How it works...

We used a base class from the *Implementing asynchronous error handling with INotifyDataErrorInfo* recipe as a starting point, providing us with an `INotifyPropertyChanged` interface implementation as a base to work on our new code.

We implemented a class derived from our `BaseClass` and created only one property, `BookRating`, of integer value. When set, it raises its `PropertyChanged` event with the `OnPropertyChanged("BookRating");` instruction.

Additionally, the setter is validated previously to a change, with a random validation method that we had set with a delay of 200 ms. With this we can simulate a long running process, a call to a service, or both.

We have to be careful with some of the issues involved: for example, if the running time of the process and validation is not fixed, a setter launched later that runs faster would execute the setter before the previous call. Additionally, there are some controls that are constantly launching events. The movement of the `Slider` control generates a constantly changing value, or `MouseMove`, which typically raises a lot of events.

These cases had to be handled previously with a technique called **throttling**, which was not easy to implement. The introduction of **RX** (**Reactive Extensions**) was an improvement, as we could do things such as:

```
Observable.FromEvent<PropertyChangedEventArgs>(x => this.
PropertyChanged +=x, x => this.PropertyChanged -= x)
    .Where(x => x.PropertyName == "NameOfSlider")
    .Select(_ => this.NameOfSlider)
    .Throttle(TimeSpan.FromMilliseconds(50));
```

Now, we can implement this in an even easier way.

 For more information on RX we recommend the official source at http://msdn.microsoft.com/en-us/data/gg577609.aspx.

Next, we created our UI, with two sliders and a textbox to display the value. We set one of the sliders with the delay attribute and the other without it:

```
<TextBox TextWrapping="Wrap" Text="{Binding BookRating, Mode=TwoWay}"
Grid.Column="1" Grid.Row="3" IsReadOnly="True" />
<Slider x:Name="SliderNotDelayed"
        Value="{Binding BookRating, Mode=TwoWay}"
        Grid.Column="1" Grid.Row="1" Margin="3" Maximum="100" />
<Slider x:Name="SliderDelayed"
        Value="{Binding BookRating, Mode=TwoWay, Delay=200}"
        Grid.Column="1" Grid.Row="2" Margin="3"
```

This `Delay` variable is in fact the throttling delay. I recommend the curious readers to explore some more and remember this parameter as a throttling delay instead of a simple delay. Its meaning and function becomes clearer and it becomes easier to remember what it does.

LiveShaping – repositioning elements when its bound data changes

With WPF 4.0, when an item in a collection was added or removed, the `CollectionView` interface that it belonged to had its filtering, sorting, and ordering updated. However, this did not happen when we modified one of its item's properties.

Now, with WPF 4.5, we can implement this behavior in real-time with the new `ICollectionViewLiveShaping` interface, so if the data is updated, so will its filtering, sorting, and ordering. Let's see how it's done.

Getting ready

In order to use this recipe you should have Visual Studio 2012 installed.

How to do it...

Here we are going to see how to implement the `ICollectionViewLiveShaping` interface to make our collection update its sorting of the collection of data and will make it change over time as well.

1. First open Visual Studio 2012 and create a new project. We will select the **WPF Application** template from the **Visual C#** category and name it `WPFLiveShaping`.

2. We will add the `BaseClass.cs` from the *Implementing asynchronous error handling with INotifyDataErrorInfo* recipe, which provides an implementation of the `INotifyDataErrorInfo` and the `INotifyPropertyChanged` interfaces.

3. Add a class and name it `BookModel.cs`, adding the following code:

```
public class BooksModel : BaseClass
{
    private string name;
    public string Name
    {
        get { return name; }
        set
        {
            name = value;
            OnPropertyChanged("Name");
        }
    }

    private String isbn;
    public String ISBN
    {
        get { return isbn; }
        set {
            isbn = value;
            OnPropertyChanged("ISBN");
        }
    }

    private Double bookPrice;
    public Double BookPrice
    {
        get { return bookPrice; }
        set {
            bookPrice = value;
            OnPropertyChanged("BookPrice");
        }
    }
}
```

4. Add the following code to the `MainWindow.xaml.cs` class:

```
public partial class MainWindow : Window
{
    public ObservableCollection<BooksModel> myBooks { get; set; }
    DispatcherTimer dt = new DispatcherTimer();
    public ICollectionViewLiveShaping cvls;
```

```csharp
public MainWindow()
{
    InitializeComponent();

    InitializeData();
    BindData();
    StartUpdatingData();
}

private void InitializeData()
{
    myBooks = new ObservableCollection<BooksModel>();
    Random r = new Random(DateTime.Now.Millisecond);

    for (int i = 0; i < 15; i++)
    {
        BooksModel bm = new BooksModel() {
                BookPrice = r.Next(1, 10),
                ISBN = i.ToString(),
                Name = "Book N°" + i.ToString()
        };

        myBooks.Add(bm);
    }
}

private void BindData()
{
    cvls = (ICollectionViewLiveShaping)CollectionViewSource.
GetDefaultView(myBooks);
    cvls.IsLiveSorting = true;
    liveShapingDataGrid.ItemsSource = (IEnumerable)cvls;
}

private void StartUpdatingData()
{
    dt.Tick += dt_Tick;
    dt.Interval = new TimeSpan(0, 0, 0, 0, 500);
    dt.Start();
}
```

```
    void dt_Tick(object sender, EventArgs e)
    {
        foreach (BooksModel bm in myBooks)
        {
            Random r = new Random(DateTime.Now.Millisecond);
            bm.BookPrice = r.Next(1, 10);
        }
    }
}
```

5. On the `MainWindow.xaml` class, we will add two `DataGrid` controls that split the view vertically with the following XAML code:

```xml
<Grid>
    <Grid.ColumnDefinitions>
        <ColumnDefinition/>
    </Grid.ColumnDefinitions>
    <Grid.RowDefinitions>
        <RowDefinition Height="30"/>
        <RowDefinition/>
    </Grid.RowDefinitions>
    <DataGrid x:Name="liveShapingDataGrid"
                AutoGenerateColumns="False"
                IsReadOnly="True" Margin="0,30,0.4,0.4" Grid.
RowSpan="2">
        <DataGrid.Columns>
            <DataGridTextColumn Header="Name" Binding="{Binding
Name}" Width="90"/>
            <DataGridTextColumn Header="ISBN" Binding="{Binding
ISBN}" Width="60"/>
            <DataGridTextColumn Header="Price" Binding="{Binding
BookPrice}" Width="50" />
        </DataGrid.Columns>
    </DataGrid>
    <Label Content="DataGrid With LiveShaping" FontWeight="Bold"
Margin="0,0,0.4,0.4"/>
</Grid>
```

6. Execute the application and click on the **Price** header on the `DataGrid`, so it gets ordered in an ascending way. Notice that the ordering of the elements is updated live as the values change, as shown in the following screenshot:

MainWindow			
DataGrid With LiveShaping			
Name	ISBN	Price	
Book Nº1	1	1	
Book Nº5	5	1	
Book Nº4	4	1	
Book Nº3	3	1	
Book Nº2	2	1	
Book Nº0	0	1	
Book Nº13	13	6	
Book Nº12	12	6	
Book Nº14	14	6	
Book Nº11	11	6	
Book Nº10	10	6	
Book Nº8	8	6	
Book Nº7	7	6	
Book Nº6	6	6	
Book Nº9	9	6	

How it works...

We started by creating a `BooksModel` class with a double `BookPrice` property.

Next, in the `MainWindow.xaml` code, we created an `ObservableCollection` interface of `BooksModel` entities, which we initialized and populated with a few elements on the `InitializeData()` method.

We did our magic on the `BindData()` method, getting the default `CollectionView` from our `ObservableCollection` and casting it as `ICollectionViewLiveShaping`, with the following instruction:

```
cvls = (ICollectionViewLiveShaping)CollectionViewSource.
GetDefaultView(myBooks);
```

We enabled the real-time sorting for the resulting `ICollectionViewLiveShaping` interface. Next, we set it as `ItemsSource` of `DataGrid`, casting this `CollectionViewLiveShaping` interface into an `IEnumerable`.

We then created the `StartUpdatingData()` method, configuring `DispatcherTimer` to run every half second and update the price of the books, so we could see some action, live from `DataGrid`. The method simply runs over all the `BooksModel` elements and updates their price with a random generated value.

There is nothing special about the view, we just created `DataGrid` to display the three properties of `BookModel`.

Finally, we executed the application, ordered the `DataGrid` by its price header, and let the real-time ordering happen live. We could observe how the ordering reacts to the property changes taking place every half second through our dispatcher timer.

There's more...

It would be interesting to explore the other options of the `ICollectionViewLiveShaping` interface, such as `IsLiveFiltering` and `IsLiveGrouping`.

We also have the option of changing how the collection behaves. It is possible to deactivate its `LiveFiltering`, `LiveGrouping`, and `LiveSorting` options with the `CanChangeLiveFiltering`, `CanChangeLiveSorting`, and `CanChangeLiveGrouping` properties.

This interface is implemented by the `ListCollectionView`, `BindingListCollectionView`, `ItemCollection`, and `CollectionViewSource` classes by default, thanks to WPF 4.5.

7
Applying the New WCF Features

In this chapter, we will cover:

- ▸ Using the asynchronous features of WCF
- ▸ Using WebSockets
- ▸ Using Contract First development

Introduction

WCF 4.5 focuses on simplicity and ease of use. One of the features that supports this statement is its streamlining of generated configuration files that have ceased to showcase default values, reducing their size greatly. Configuring the ASP.NET compatibility is also easier since WCF configuration files are validated by Visual Studio 2012 as part of the build process. It has also improved in HTTPS protocol mapping and increased designer functionalities, such as XML editor tooltips.

Other additions include Contract First development, asynchronous streaming support, and WebSockets support.

Using the asynchronous features of WCF

One issue with the previous versions of WCF was that its service contracts did not contain definitions of its asynchronous members, resulting in unnecessary complexity in the WCF code when using asynchronous calls. Furthermore, the code was prone to timeouts and error-handling issues.

There are some scenarios that require these kinds of asynchronous calls:

- ► Executing multiple requests in parallel and continuing when they have finished.

- ► Executing a sequence of requests and stopping if one of them fails.

- ► Performing a hierarchy of operations that can occur sequentially, and also executing various requests in parallel after a given one. This is, in effect, a combination of the previous two types.

WCF 4.5 simplifies this behavior and also makes the web services easily testable.

Next, we will explore how to implement an asynchronous web service and consume it.

Getting ready

In order to use this recipe, you should have Visual Studio 2012 installed.

How to do it...

In this recipe, we will explore the new asynchronous features of WCF.

1. First, open Visual Studio 2012, create a new project by navigating to **Visual C# |
   Web**, and use the **ASP.NET Empty Web Application** template to create a web project
   to host the web service. Name it `WebAppWcfAsyncHost` and click on **OK**.

2. Right-click on the project and add a new item of the type **WCF Service**; name it
   `AsyncService.svc` and click on the **Add** button.

3. Open the generated `IAsyncService.cs` file and replace the code with the following:

```
[ServiceContract]
public interface IAsyncService
{
    [OperationContract]
    Task<int> DoWorkAsync();
}
```

4. Note that we will have to add a reference to `System.Threading.Tasks`.

5. Open the `AsyncService` class and replace the code with the following:

```
public class AsyncService : IAsyncService
{
    Public async Task<int> DoWorkAsync()
    {
        return new System.Random().Next(1, 10);
    }
}
```

6. Build the application.

7. Add a new project by navigating to **Visual C# | Windows**, and select the **Console Application** template. Name it `ConsoleWcfServiceAsyncConsumer` and click on the **OK** button.

8. Set it as the startup project.

9. Right-click on the newly added project and select **Add Service Reference**.

10. Click on the **Discover** button and the provided service should appear; select it and in the **Namespace** field write `AsyncServiceReference`, as shown in the following screenshot, and click on the **OK** button.

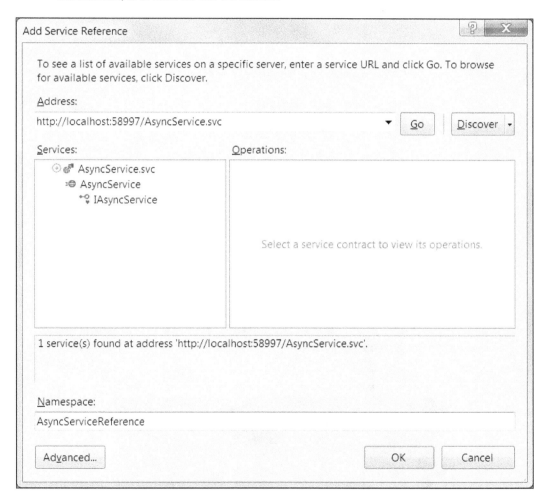

11. Open the `Program.cs` file in the designer and enter the following code:

```
class Program
{
    Static AsyncServiceClient svcCli = new AsyncServiceClient();

    static void Main(string[] args)
    {
        Console.WriteLine("Requesting values");
        var result = GetResultsFromWebService();
        Console.WriteLine("The result is: " + result.Result.
        ToString());
        Console.ReadLine();
    }

    Static async Task<int> GetResultsFromWebService()
    {
        var t1 = svcCli.DoWorkAsync();
        var t2 = svcCli.DoWorkAsync();
        var t3 = svcCli.DoWorkAsync();
        var t4 = svcCli.DoWorkAsync();

        Console.WriteLine("Waiting for all the values to be
        returned..");
        await Task.WhenAll(t1, t2, t3, t4);

        Console.WriteLine("All the values received,
        processing..");
        return t1.Result + t2.Result + t3.Result + t4.Result;
    }
}
```

12. Press the *F5* key to start executing the program. We should see the result of our program in the console as shown in the following image:

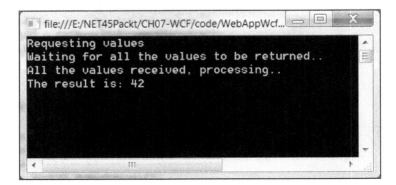

13. We have just created an asynchronous WCF service, called it asynchronously many times, and synchronized the reception of the different web service calls.

How it works...

Essentially, the only different thing we did was to add the `Task<int>` command to the `WebService` method declaration; the rest simply works out of the box.

On the client side, we called our random asynchronous value provider four times and assigned the results to the tasks. We then used the `Task.WhenAll()` method to wait for the tasks, so the code will not continue running this method until all the tasks have finished; this means that all the web service calls have returned.

Although this example might seem simple, imagine that you changed the random integer services with other possible services, such as `GetOrderTotal`, `GetOrderTaxes`, or `GetOrderShippingCosts`, and you will begin to see the possibilities. This new coding style simplifies our code noticeably, and makes it easier to maintain and understand.

The **Task-Based Asynchronous Pattern** that we have just seen is clearly superior to and simpler than the previous event-based patterns and `IASyncResult` asynchronous patterns.

We should use this pattern as the preferred way to implement any WCF asynchronous operation.

It is also important to keep in mind that the use of this pattern is beneficial for scalability since it assures that thread-related resources are only consumed when the code is being executed. An asynchronous solution will allow the thread resources to be used by other means while waiting for I/O, database operations, or other services to complete. When the operation is complete, it will yield the necessary data for the operation to continue.

See also

Look into the *Understanding async and await in .NET 4.5* recipe of *Chapter 2, Exploring the Top New Features of the CLR*, dedicated to CLR and the usage of `async` and `await`.

Using WebSockets

WebSockets are bidirectional, full-duplex channels that start as HTTP channels and use handshakes to upgrade the channels to WebSockets, with real, two-way TCP communication between the client and the server. The added benefit is that all of this can happen through port 80 and that they are router friendly.

In this recipe, we will see how to create and consume a WebSockets service.

Getting ready

In order to use this recipe, you should have Windows 8 with Visual Studio 2012 installed. WebSockets are only supported natively on Windows 8; see `http://msdn.microsoft.com/en-us/library/hh159285.aspx`.

How to do it...

Here, we are going to set up our system in order to support WebSockets and implement a basic WebSocket.

1. First, we need to validate that the following Windows features are installed on our Windows 8 machine:

   - ASP.NET 4.5 and HTTP activation
   - WebSockets over Internet Information Services

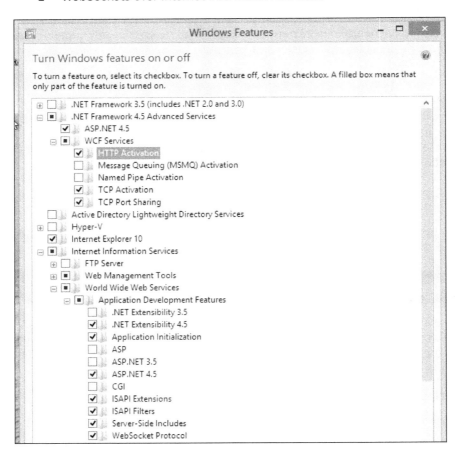

2. Open Visual Studio 2012; create a new project by navigating to **Visual C# | Web** and use the **ASP.NET Empty Web Application** template to create a web project to host the web service. Name it `WebSocketsWcf` and click on the **OK** button.

3. Right-click on the project and add a new item of the type **WCF Service**; then name it `WebSocketsService.svc` and click on the **Add** button.

4. Open the generated `IWebSocketsService.cs` file and replace the code with the following:

```
[ServiceContract(CallbackContract = typeof(IWebSocketsServiceCallb
ack))]
public interface IWebSocketsService
{
    [OperationContract(IsOneWay = true)]
    Task StartSendingData();
}
```

5. Note that we will have to add a reference to `System.Threading.Tasks` to add support for asynchronous operations and types.

6. We will get an indication for the `IWebSocketsServiceCallback` exception, which we will solve on the next step.

7. Create a `IWebSocketsServiceCallback.cs` class and add the following code:

```
  [ServiceContract]
public interface IWebSocketsServiceCallback
{
    [OperationContract(IsOneWay = true)]
    Task SendData(string data);
}
```

8. Note that we have to add a `usings` clause for `System.Threading.Tasks` and for the `System.ServiceModel` namespaces.

9. Open the `WebSocketsService.svc.cs` file and substitute the following for the code:

```
public class WebSocketsService : IWebSocketsService
{
public async Task StartSendingData()
    {
Var callbackFunction = OperationContext.Current.GetCallbackChannel
<IWebSocketsServiceCallback>();

while ((callbackFunction as IChannel).State == CommunicationState.
Opened)
```

```
            {
await callbackFunction.SendData("Hi, the time is : " + DateTime.
Now.ToLongTimeString());
await Task.Delay(5000);
            }
        }
}
```

10. At this point, we need to add a reference to `System.Threading.Tasks` and `System.ServiceModel.Channnels`.

11. Edit the `Web.Config` file and substitute the following for the code:

```
<?xml version="1.0"?>
<configuration>
<appSettings>
<add key="aspnet:UseTaskFriendlySynchronizationContext"
value="true" />
</appSettings>
<system.web>
<compilation debug="true" targetFramework="4.5" />
<httpRuntimetargetFramework="4.5" />
</system.web>

<system.serviceModel>
<protocolMapping>
<add scheme="http" binding="netHttpBinding" />
<add scheme="https" binding="netHttpsBinding" />
</protocolMapping>
<behaviors>
<serviceBehaviors>
<behavior name="">
<serviceMetadatahttpGetEnabled="true" httpsGetEnabled="true" />
<serviceDebugincludeExceptionDetailInFaults="false" />
</behavior>
</serviceBehaviors>
</behaviors>
<serviceHostingEnvironmentaspNetCompatibilityEnabled="true"
multipleSiteBindingsEnabled="true" />
</system.serviceModel>
</configuration>
```

12. Build the application.

13. Add a new project by navigating to **Visual C#** | **Windows** and selecting the **Console Application** template. Name it `WebSocketsConsoleClient` and press the **OK** button.

14. Set it as the startup project.

15. Right-click on the newly added project and select **Add Service Reference**.

16. Click on the **Discover** button and the recently defined WebSockets service should appear. Select it, and in the **Namespace** parameter type `WebSocketsServiceReference` and press the **OK** button.

17. Add a new class named **WebSocketsCallbackHandler** to the console project with the following code:

```
class WebSocketsCallBackHandler : WebSocketsServiceReference.
IWebSocketsServiceCallback
{
    public void SendData(string data)
    {
        Console.WriteLine("Received data from the WebSockets
        service: " + data);
    }
}
```

18. Continue by opening the `Program.cs` file and substituting the main method with the following code:

```
static void Main(string[] args)
{
    try
    {
        Var InstanceCtx = new InstanceContext
        (new WebSocketsCallBackHandler());
        Var WebSocketsClient = new WebSocketsServiceReference.
        WebSocketsServiceClient(InstanceCtx);

        WebSocketsClient.StartSendingData();

        Console.ReadLine();

    }
    catch (Exception ex)
    {

    throw;
    }
}
```

19. We have to add a `using` clause for the `System.ServiceModel` namespace.

20. Open the `App.config` file that was autogenerated when we added the service reference, and validate that the endpoint definition has its binding set to **netHttpBinding**.

21. Now let's build and execute our solution; if all goes well, we should see the following result on our console:

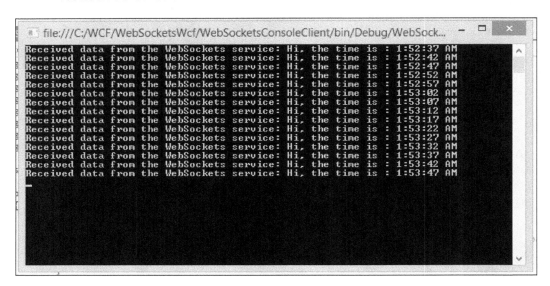

22. And that's it; we just created a WebSockets WCF service and a client that consumes it!

How it works...

First, we configured our Windows 8 operating system to support WebSockets, ASP.NET 4.5, and HTTP activation features. It is necessary to have .NET 4.5 on the operating system, either by installing it automatically when performing the installation of Visual Studio 2012 or by installing it as a standalone.

Note that WebSockets will not run on previous operating systems that don't have IIS8 installed, so this feature is unsupported natively on Windows 7.

We created an ASP.NET web app to host our web service and added the following attribute to it:

```
[ServiceContract(CallbackContract = typeof(IWebSocketsServiceCallba
ck))]
```

Essentially, we are defining `ServiceContract` and setting up `IWebSocketsServiceCallback` as the callback context.

Then on the interface, we added just one method, `StartSendingData()`, with the attribute:

```
[OperationContract(IsOneWay = true)]
```

This indicates that this method will only move in one direction, that is, from the client to the server. We are going to use it as a handshake that will set up the communication between the client and the server.

Note that we are using *tasks*, so this will comply with the `async/await` model that .NET 4.5 can be proud of.

Next we have created `IWebSocketsServiceCallback`, which is also a service contract, where we defined the `SendData()` method task that we set to follow a one-way route. We will obviously use this to send data which the clients usually updates. Note that we need to implement this on the client too, for this to work properly.

To continue, we need to implement the interfaces we just defined. For `WebSocketsService`, we set up the `StartSendingData()` method that gets the current callback channel. While the channel is open, we keep on executing asynchronous calls to the callback method.

In order to finish the server part, we use `configuredWeb.Config` where we have added a protocol mapping for HTTP and HTTPS to `netHttpBinding/netHttpBindings`, which we will use for our WCF endpoints.

We built the project and added a console application that will be the client of our service. In the console application, we had to add a service reference to our recently created web service.

We created a class called `WebSocketsCallBackHandler` to hold our implementation of the callback method. The received data is redirected to the console with a `WriteLine` command.

In our main method, we'll create an instance of this class with the callback handler class as its parameter, thus generating a client for our web service. From the following instance, we just call the *handshake* method that will trigger the server to start sending data.

```
Var InstanceCtx = new InstanceContext(new
WebSocketsCallBackHandler());
Var WebSocketsClient = new WebSocketsServiceReference.WebSocketsServic
eClient(InstanceCtx);
WebSocketsClient.StartSendingData();
```

And that's all there is to it! Notice how, despite its power, the solution is extremely simple.

Using Contract First development

Contract First development comes to us in .NET 4.5 WCF as the ability to create the service interface and data contract from a WSDL file. The WSDL file is generated in the `svcutil.exe` application with the `/servicecontract` flag.

This provides an excellent way to parallelize development since we can work on the backend service while it is being constructed, given that the service requirements and contract have been defined beforehand.

In this recipe, we will see how to use this new feature.

Getting ready

In order to use this recipe, you should have Visual Studio 2012 installed and a WSDL contract. For this recipe, we will use the dynamically generated web service we implemented in the first recipe.

How to do it...

In this recipe, we are going to generate a client for a WSDL file.

1. Open the project of our first recipe and set the ASP.NET website that hosts the asynchronous web service. Navigate on the browser to the web service, appending `?wsdl` to the address. You should get something like `http://localhost:58997/AsyncService.svc?wsdl`. Note that the port might change. It will generate an XML file with the WSDL definition and display it in our browser as follows:

2. Navigate to your `Visual Studio tools` folder and open the `VS2012 Tools` command prompt corresponding to your CPU.

3. Navigate to where you want to generate the service code.

4. Type the following command, noting that the port might change:

   `svcutil /sc http://localhost:58997/AsyncService.svc?wsdl`

5. Note that we used the reduced form `/sc` of the `/servicecontract` flag on our command.

6. We should get a notification that `ASyncService.cs` has been generated, as we can see in the following screenshot:

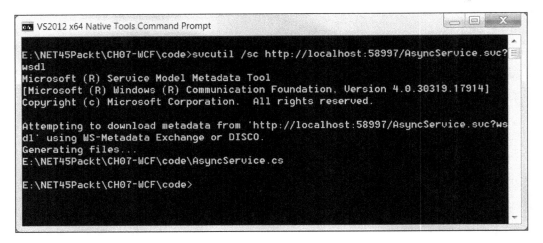

7. We could accomplish this with a WDSL file, with or without an XSD file.

8. We will find our service contract in the file that was generated by our command prompt, which is `AsyncServices.cs` in our case.

9. This file should contain the following code:

```
//------------------------------------------------------------
//--------------
// <auto-generated>
//     This code was generated by a tool.
//     Runtime Version:4.0.30319.17914
//
//     Changes to this file may cause incorrect behavior and will
be lost if
//     the code is regenerated.
// </auto-generated>
//------------------------------------------------------------
//--------------

 [System.CodeDom.Compiler.GeneratedCodeAttribute("System.
ServiceModel", "4.0.0.0")]
 [System.ServiceModel.ServiceContractAttribute(ConfigurationName="I
AsyncService")]
 public interface IAsyncService
```

```
{
     [System.ServiceModel.OperationContractAttribute(Action="h
ttp://tempuri.org/IAsyncService/DoWork", ReplyAction="http://
tempuri.org/IAsyncService/DoWorkResponse")]
Int DoWork();
}
```

10. If we had any data elements, they would also have been generated.

11. This technique allows us to generate a client that works against a given service implementation.

How it works...

This recipe is quite straightforward; after getting the WSDL file for our web service, all it takes is for us to use the svcutil tool to generate the service interface and the data contract.

8

Creating and Hosting Our First ASP.NET Web API

In this chapter we will cover:

- ▶ Creating our first ASP.NET web API
- ▶ Implementing a CRUD ASP.NET web API
- ▶ Setting up a self-hosted ASP.NET web API

Introduction

.NET 4.5 introduces the capability to create ASP.NET web APIs. This is brought to us by **ASP. NET MVC4**. Basically, the ASP.NET web API is a framework that enables developers to easily build HTTP services. This makes the framework a good fit to build **RESTful** applications over .NET 4.5.

An important point is that, since these services are being exposed over HTTP, we can integrate them with almost any client device and technology in the market, which makes them extremely useful.

ASP.NET web APIs provide support for:

- A modern HTTP programming model, allowing direct access and manipulation of HTTP requests and responses.

- Content negotiation, which helps determine the proper format for the data that the ASP.NET Web API returns. JSON and XML are supported out of the box and customizations for our own formats and structures are also allowed.

- Query composition through **OData** conventions, supporting OData queries automatically out of the box when we return `IQueryable<T>` from our ASP.NET web API methods.

- Model binding, providing them directly on an HTTP request, and converting them into .NET objects.

- Self-hosting.

ASP.NET web API adds more punch with coding features such as routing capabilities support, testability additions, **IoC,** and more.

In the following sections we will see how to create our first ASP.NET web API, create a CRUD with it, and explore its self-hosting option.

Creating our first ASP.NET web API

In this recipe, we will see how to expose a basic service and some data through HTTP with the ASP.NET web API.

Getting ready

In order to use this recipe, you should have Visual Studio 2012 and ASP.NET MVC 4 installed (the latter one includes the ASP.NET web API).

How to do it...

Next we are going to create a web API:

1. To start, open Visual Studio 2012, select the web category from the visual C# categories and use the **ASP.NET MVC 4 Web Application** template to create a new project. Name it `WebAPI101`.

2. On the **New ASP.NET MVC 4 Project** dialog select the **Web API** template and click on the **OK** button.

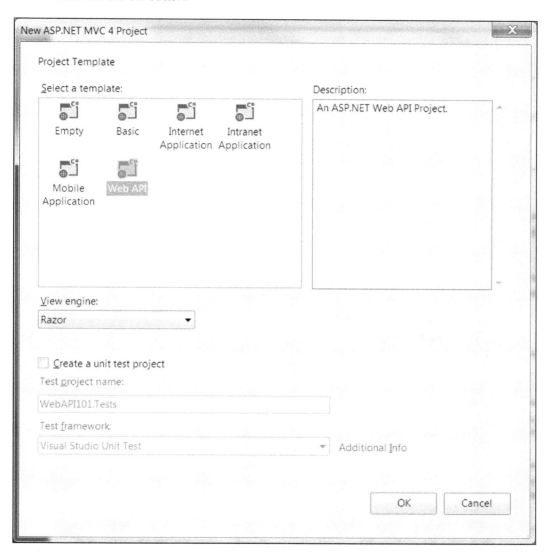

The following project structure will be created for us:

3. In the `Models` folder we will add a class, name it `Booksmodel.cs`, and introduce the following code:

```
public class BookModel
{
Public int Id { get; set; }
public String Title { get; set; }
public String Description { get; set; }
public bool IsOnSale { get; set; }
public int BookRating { get; set; }
public double BookPrice { get; set; }
}
```

4. Next, we will add our own controller; right-click on the `Controllers` folder, select **Add**, and then left-click over the **Controller...** option, as shown in the following screenshot:

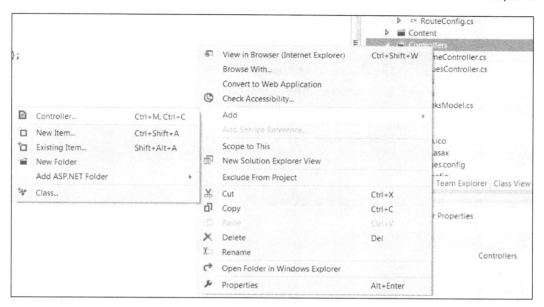

5. In the **Controller** dialog in **Add**, give it the name `BooksController`, select the **Empty API Controller** template, and click on the **Add** button.

6. We could have started by opening the `ValuesController.cs` file and customizing it, but it is better to delete this file so that we can illustrate the entire process.

7. Open the `BooksController.cs` file and change the code of the `BooksController` class to the following:

```
public class BooksController : ApiController
{
    BookModel[] Books = null;
    public BooksController()
    {
        Books = GenerateBooks();
    }
    public IEnumerable<BookModel> Get()
    {
        return Books;
    }
    public BookModel Get(int id)
    {
        var book = (from b in Books
                    where b.Id == id
                    select b).FirstOrDefault();
        return book;
    }
    private BookModel[] GenerateBooks() {
        BookModel[] Books = new BookModel[] {
            new BookModel(){
                Id=1,
                Title = ".NET 4.5 First Look",
                Description = "A book to quickly and
practically get into .NET 4.5"
            },
            new BookModel(){
                Id=2,
                Title = "The lost book of Agatha Christie",
                Description = "A book everybody wants to
read..."
            }
        };
        return Books;
    }
}
```

8. Press *F5* to debug the application.

9. In the URL, add `api/books/`, so it will look similar to `http://localhost:19347/api/books/` and press *Enter*. Please note that the port number might change.

10. If we are opening the web page with Internet Explorer, we should see the following message:

Do you want to open or save **books** (306 bytes) from **localhost**?   Open   Save ▼   Cancel   ×

11. We will open it with Notepad, and our content will be as follows:

```
[{"Id":1,"Title":".NET 4.5 First Look","Description":"A book to
quickly and practically get into .NET 4.5","IsOnSale":false,"BookR
ating":0,"BookPrice":0.0},{"Id":2,"Title":"The lost book of Agatha
Christie","Description":"A book everybody wants to read...","IsOnS
ale":false,"BookRating":0,"BookPrice":0.0}]
```

12. This is the response from our web API. If we open it with another browser, such as Mozilla Firefox or Google Chrome, we will see it as an XML visualization:

```
This XML file does not appear to have any style information associated with it. The document tree is shown below.

▼<ArrayOfBookModel xmlns:i="http://www.w3.org/2001/XMLSchema-instance"
  xmlns="http://schemas.datacontract.org/2004/07/WebAPI101.Models">
 ▼<BookModel>
    <BookPrice>0</BookPrice>
    <BookRating>0</BookRating>
  ▼<Description>
     A book to quickly and practically get into .NET 4.5
    </Description>
    <Id>1</Id>
    <IsOnSale>false</IsOnSale>
    <Title>.NET 4.5 First Look</Title>
  </BookModel>
 ▼<BookModel>
    <BookPrice>0</BookPrice>
    <BookRating>0</BookRating>
    <Description>A book everybody wants to read...</Description>
    <Id>2</Id>
    <IsOnSale>false</IsOnSale>
    <Title>The lost book of Agatha Christie</Title>
  </BookModel>
</ArrayOfBookModel>
```

13. Note that to run it on another browser, we have to expand the browser dropdown located on the **DEBUG** button, as follows:

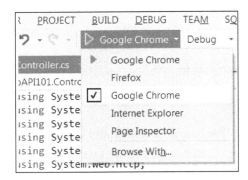

14. The response is so browser dependent because our web API is sending different content types due to the **Accept** section in the request headers. We are getting a JSON response for IE and an XML response for other browsers.

15. An interesting step here would be to test the browser tools (for Internet Explorer and for Google Chrome) and see the http network traffic, specifically the request headers and returned types for each browser.

16. We could go on and explore the web API to get a single book, filtering by its ID. Execute the application with Firefox, go to the URL, add `api/books/1` to it, so it will look similar to `http://localhost:19347/api/books/1`, and press *Enter*. We should get the following response:

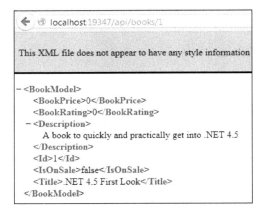

With these few steps we have created a very simple ASP.NET Web API and tested it with a browser.

How it works...

We created an ASP.NET web API from its ASP.NET MVC 4 template, where we built a model to define the information to be exposed through the web API, and then went on to create the controller.

A web API controller is derived from the `ApiController` class. Its main function is to prepare, filter, and return the requested information.

It is important to note the routing concept in web API, where there is a mapping of the URL to the methods we expose in the controller class, resulting in the routes:

- ▶ `/api/Books:Get()`
- ▶ `/api/Books:Get(1)`

If we explore the `RouteConfig.cs` file, in the `App_Start` folder, we will observe that some mappings have been added, such as `api/{controller}/{id}`, where `{controller}` and `{id}` are placeholders.

The mapping process works as follows: the web API framework decides which API controller will handle the request by matching `{placeholder}` to the controller's name. Then the placeholder `{id}` is matched to a parameter of the same name.

In our case, `Books` is matched to `BooksController`. Since the request is a `GET`, it looks for a method that starts with `Get` and has no parameters; therefore, it is matched to `Get()`. However, we could have given it the name `GetBooks()` or `GetAllBooks()` and the result would have been the same. Finally, when we put in an extra parameter for the ID, the web API framework looks for a matching `GET` method that has an ID parameter, which matches our `Get(int id)` as a result.

Next, we have created the GenerateBooks() method, which we call on the constructor of our BooksController class, the Get() method that returns the whole array of books, and the Get(int id) function that returns only the book with the requested ID.

We have tested our web API from our browser, to get the full list of books and then a specific book.

There's more...

This is of course a very basic view of the web API and we have left plenty of interesting areas to explore, such as creating web API clients, routing and actions, custom formats, model binding, hosting aspects, OData support, extensibility features, testing, and debugging capabilities.

See also

- ► *Implementing a CRUD ASP.NET Web API*
- ► *Setting up a self-hosted ASP.NET Web API*

Implementing a CRUD ASP.NET web API

In this recipe, we will see how to create an ASP.NET web API that supports **CRUD** operations, which stands for **Create Read Update and Delete**. These map to the standard database operations that correspond to the following HTTP verbs:

- ► GET: The GET method retrieves whatever information is identified by the requesting URI
- ► PUT: The PUT method requests that the enclosed entity is to be stored under the supplied requesting URI
- ► POST: The POST method requests that the enclosed entity is to be a subordinate of the resource identified by the requesting URI
- ► DELETE: The DELETE method requests that the resource identified by the requesting URI should be deleted

In this recipe, we will see how to implement these CRUD features on the previously created service, with the HTTP verbs, and the ASP.NET web API.

Getting ready

In order to use this recipe, you should have Visual Studio 2012 and ASP.NET MVC 4 installed (the latter one includes the ASP.NET web API). You should also have the project resulting from our previous recipe.

How to do it...

Here we are going to implement the CRUD verbs into the web API that we created in our previous section:

1. Copy our previous recipe project into a new folder and name it `WebAPICRUD`.

2. Create a class with the name of `IRepository.cs` with the following code:

```
public interface IRepository<T> where T : class
{
    IEnumerable<T> GetAll();
    T GetById(int id);
    void Insert(T entity);
    void Update(T entity);
    void Delete(T entity);
}
```

3. Add a class named `BooksRepository.cs` containing the following code:

```
public class BooksRepository : IRepository<BookModel>
{
    ObservableCollection<BookModel> ocBooks = null;
    public BooksRepository()
    {
        ocBooks = GenerateBooks();
    }
    private ObservableCollection<BookModel> GenerateBooks()
    {
        ObservableCollection<BookModel> Books = new ObservableColl
ection<BookModel>() {
            new BookModel(){
                    Id=1,
                    Title = ".NET 4.5 First Look",
                    Description = "A book to quickly and
practically get into .NET 4.5"
            },
            new BookModel(){
```

```
                        Id=2,
                        Title = "The lost book of Agatha Christie",
                        Description = "A book everybody wants to
read..."
                    }
            };
            return Books;
        }
        public IEnumerable<BookModel> GetAll() {
            return ocBooks;
        }
        public BookModel GetById(int id) {
            var book = (from b in ocBooks
                        where b.Id == id
                        select b).FirstOrDefault();
            return book;
        }
        public void Insert(BookModel book) {
            book.Id = GetLatestIdPlusOne();
            ocBooks.Add(book);
        }
        private int GetLatestIdPlusOne()
        {
            int BiggestId = 0;
            foreach (BookModel book in ocBooks)
            {
                if (BiggestId < book.Id) {
                    BiggestId = book.Id;
                }
            }
            return (BiggestId + 1);
        }
        public void Update(BookModel book) {
            this.Delete(book);
            ocBooks.Add(book);
        }
        public void Delete(BookModel book) {
            BookModel bookToRemove = GetById(book.Id);
            ocBooks.Remove(bookToRemove);
        }
    }
}
```

4. And substitute the following code for our `BooksController.cs` content:

```
public class BooksController : ApiController
{
    static readonly IRepository<BookModel> BooksRep =
        new BooksRepository();
    public IEnumerable<BookModel> Get()
    {
        return BooksRep.GetAll();
    }
    public HttpResponseMessage Get(int id)
    {
        BookModel bm = BooksRep.GetById(id);
        if (bm != null)
        {
            return Request.CreateResponse<BookModel>(HttpStatusCo
de.OK, bm);
        }
        else {
            return Request.CreateResponse<BookModel>(HttpStatusCo
de.NotFound, null);
        }
    }
    public void Put(BookModel bm) {
        BooksRep.Update(bm);
        HttpResponseMessage hrm = Request.CreateResponse<BookModel
>(HttpStatusCode.Created, bm);
    }
    public HttpResponseMessage Post(BookModel bm)
    {
        BooksRep.Insert(bm);
        HttpResponseMessage hrm = Request.CreateResponse<BookModel
>(HttpStatusCode.Created, bm);
        hrm.Headers.Location = new Uri(Url.Link("DefaultApi", new
{ id = bm.Id }));
        return hrm;
    }
    public HttpResponseMessage Delete(BookModel bm)
    {
        BooksRep.Delete(bm);
```

```
                return new HttpResponseMessage(HttpStatusCode.NoContent);
            }
        }
```

5. And that's it! We now have a ready to go (albeit very basic) web API that implements the main HTTP verbs.

How it works...

We started from a copy of our past web API project so we could re-use the basics.

Next we implemented the repository pattern, with the `IRepository` interface and the `BooksRepository` class. This is a good practice to increase readability and testability, even if our actual implementation is working upon an observable collection in memory. If we wanted to improve this example to use a database, for example, we would just need to slightly change the `BooksRepository` implementation of the `IRepository` interface.

On this repository, we implemented an initialization of our database, the `GetAll()` and `Get(int id)` functions and `Insert(BookModel book)` with a helper function `GetLatestIdPlusOne()` to get the largest book ID and add one to it.

We also implemented the `Update()` and `Delete()` methods.

To follow, we built the `BooksController` class, which we started from scratch. First, we added a static member of the type `IRepository<BookModel>`, associating it with a new `BooksRepository`:

```
static readonly IRepository<BookModel> BooksRep =
        new BooksRepository();
```

With this singleton in place, we can use it wherever we want from our `BooksController` class, making it global to all the instances of the `BooksController` class.

We implemented the `GET` verbs first, in a very similar way to what we had done previously. However, in the current implementation, they are now more decoupled and the responsibility of getting the element now resides with the repository.

The `PUT`, `POST`, and `DELETE` verbs were also very straightforward to implement, by calling the method directly.

Additionally, you will observe that we have been returning an adequate `HttpResponseMessage` with each of these verbs, perfectly matching what the protocol is expecting.

Setting up a self-hosted ASP.NET web API

In this recipe, we will demonstrate how to self-host an ASP.NET web API. A web API gives us the flexibility to host our web API in our process, also called self-hosting.

Getting ready

In order to use this recipe you should have Visual Studio 2012 and ASP.NET MVC 4 installed (the latter includes the ASP.NET Web API).

How to do it...

Next we are going to self-host our web API.

1. Create a new console application project and name it `WebAPISelfHosted`.

2. Open the NuGet package manager, which you can launch from the **Tools** menu, select **Library Package Manager**, and click on **Manage NuGet Packages for Solution**.

3. Select the online packages, and look for **Microsoft ASP.NET Web API Self Host** and click on **Install** as shown in the following screenshot:

4. We will add a class named `Booksmodel.cs` with the following code:

```
public class BookModel
{
    public int Id { get; set; }
```

```
        public String Title { get; set; }
        public String Description { get; set; }
        public bool IsOnSale { get; set; }
        public int BookRating { get; set; }
        public double BookPrice { get; set; }
    }
}
```

5. Next we will add a controller. Right-click on our project, select **New item** from **Add** and type `controller` there. The ASP.NET **Web API Controller Class** option will appear. Select it, name it `BooksController`, and press the **Add** button, as shown in the following screenshot:

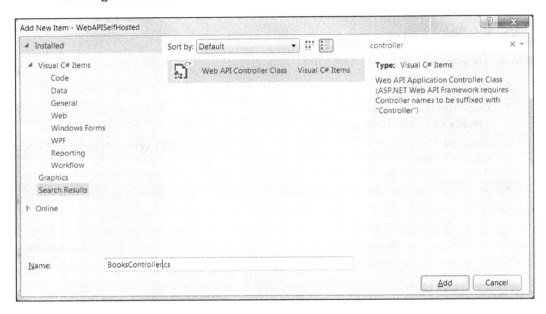

6. We will insert exactly the same code in `BooksController` as in our first controller, as follows:

```
public class BooksController : ApiController
{
    BookModel[] Books = null;
    public BooksController()
    {
        Books = GenerateBooks();
    }
    public IEnumerable<BookModel> Get()
    {
        return Books;
```

```
    }
    public BookModel Get(int id)
    {
        var book = (from b in Books
                    where b.Id == id
                    select b).FirstOrDefault();
        return book;
    }
    private BookModel[] GenerateBooks()
    {
        BookModel[] Books = new BookModel[] {
            new BookModel(){
                Id=1,
                Title = ".NET 4.5 First Look",
                Description = "A book to quickly and
practically get into .NET 4.5"
            },
            new BookModel(){
                Id=2,
                Title = "The lost book of Agatha Christie",
                Description = "A book everybody wants to
read..."
            }
        };
        return Books;
    }
}
```

7. We will open the `Programs.cs` file and add the following code:

```
static void Main(string[] args)
{
    HttpSelfHostConfiguration cfg = new HttpSelfHostConfiguration(
"http://localhost:8030");

    cfg.Routes.MapHttpRoute(
        "API Default",
        "api/{controller}/{id}",
        new { id = RouteParameter.Optional }
        );
    using (HttpSelfHostServer server = new
HttpSelfHostServer(cfg))
    {
        server.OpenAsync().Wait();
        Console.WriteLine("Press Enter to finalize the service (or
close the console application).");
        Console.ReadLine();
    }
```

8. We might get a reference problem when handling the routes; if this happens, add a reference in the project to `System.Web.Routing.dll` and to `System.Web.dll`.

9. Add a `using` clause such as the following in the `Program.cs` file:

   `Using System.Web.Http.Routing;`

10. Now save the solution, close Visual Studio 2012, and open it again as administrator.

11. Open the solution again and execute it by pressing *F5*.

12. We should see the console application being executed and waiting for us to finalize.

13. Launch a browser, Firefox for example, and type the URI that we wrote, together with the web API syntax, to get all the books: `http:// http://localhost:8030/api/Books` and press *Enter*.

14. We should see the following result:

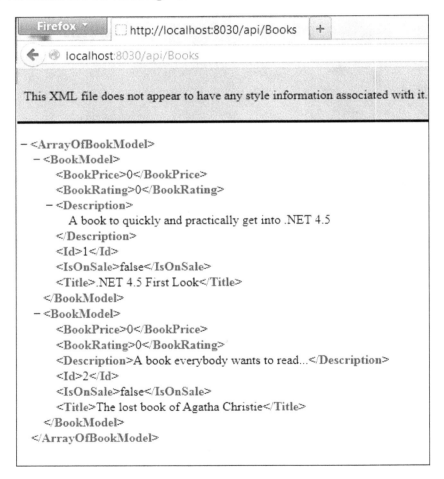

How it works...

In this recipe, we created a console application, to which we added, through NuGet, the `Microsoft ASP.NET Web API Self Host` package.

Following this, we added the `BooksModel.cs` class that we used on our first recipe and the same `BooksController.cs` class, changing the namespaces to match our current project.

We saw how to solve a possible reference problem and went into the main part of the project. In the `Program.cs` file we added the needed references and created a new `HttpSelfHostConfiguration` class with the URL that our application will service.

We mapped the route to our web API and created a server with the newly defined configuration. There we wait for an *Enter* to be hit to continue the flow and finish the application.

Additionally, we explored the web API with a browser and checked that it works as expected.

Note that in order to run this application, you will need to open Visual Studio 2012 as an administrator, since serving a specific HTTP domain on the machine requires administrator privileges. Another alternative option for this would be to reserve the URL with `Netsh.exe`, but this service does not run permanently on this machine and/or URL, so the **Run as admin** option is preferable.

9
Using the New Capabilities of WF

In this chapter, we will cover:

- ▶ Creating a state machine workflow
- ▶ Using the enhanced designer features

Introduction

WF, which stands for **Workflow Foundation**, was first presented in society almost six years ago on November 2007 as part of .NET 3.0. Now it comes to us as a greatly enhanced framework with polished features and some sweetness under its cape.

WF 4.5 has softened the edges that were still present in 4.0 and now offers a state machine workflow model, so we no longer have to simulate it with flowcharts or use the **CodePlex state machine**.

It is interesting to note that the CodePlex state machine project, which can be found at `http://wf.codeplex.com/releases/view/67992`, is a predecessor of the current state machine—it was put out as soon as WF4 was shipped to get feedback from the community early on.

It comes with many enhancements that the community has been asking for, such as C# expressions. The list of designer improvements is long: panning, search with navigable results, quick find, a document outline, autosurround with sequence, annotations, multiselection for activities, auto-connect, and auto-insert. Another useful addition is the build time workflow validation, and errors in the XAML file will now break the build. To top it off, workflow validation is executed in the background while in the designer.

We now have `WorkflowIdentity`, which basically gives us the ability to associate a name and version with a fully configured definition; identity is configured at the host level and all instances are annotated with that identity that lives through the life cycle of the activity.

We have the ability to use **side versioning** as well, where we can have multiple versions of the definitions of a workflow executing at the same time.

Additionally, we have workflow versioning called `DynamicUpdate` with dynamic update capabilities, so now we can update a persisted workflow to a newer version. It is possible to run different versions side by side.

On the activities side, we now have `NoPersistScope` and some additional capabilities, such as validating the unconnected nodes and the `DisplayName` property.

Activity templates can now be generated from the contract with the new **Contract First** development mode. This allows us to generate the operations for the contract, given that we have an existing WCF contract, to generate a set of activities to represent the operations in it. Contract First also allows us to validate a workflow; this means that if a workflow claims to have implemented a contract, it should implement all its operations as well.

This Contract First is "opt-in," so we can use the usual authoring to create activities or use Contract First.

If all of this wasn't enough, Microsoft is bringing WF to the cloud, which clearly states the importance of the .NET workflow "de facto" framework.

Finally, workflows can now be run in partially trusted application domains, obviously with less permissions and capabilities.

In the following sections, we will see how to create our first state machine workflow and how to use the main designer's new features.

Creating a state machine workflow

State machines are not a new citizen of WF but are now here to stay as a solid part of WF. They have a new type of activity, the `StateMachine` activity, with two classes to help us define a state machine: state and transition. State helps us define a state that the machine can then be in and a transition helps us define which state changes can occur from a specific state.

In this recipe, we will see how to create a state machine workflow with WF 4.5, execute it, and debug it.

Getting ready

In order to use this recipe, you should have Visual Studio 2012 installed.

How to do it...

We are going to create a state machine workflow using the following steps:

1. First open Visual Studio 2012, create a new project by navigating to **Visual C# | Workflow**, and use the **Workflow Console Application** template to create a new project. Name it `WFStateMachine` and click on **Ok**.

2. Close the `Workflow1.xaml` file that will open on creating the project and rename it to `MyStateMachine.xaml`. To do this, we can right-click and select **Rename** or select it with a click and press *F2*.

3. Open `Program.cs` and change the `Workflow1` reference to our new name, `MyStateMachine`. We can also change the instance name to match the new name, as in the following code:

```
class Program
{
static void Main(string[] args)
    {
        // Create and cache the workflow definition
        Activity MyStateMachineInstance = new MyStateMachine();
WorkflowInvoker.Invoke(MyStateMachineInstance);
    }
```

4. Note that the `MyStateMachine` class appears in red, so we still need to make a minor change. Right-click on **onMyStateMachine** and select the **view code** option.

5. On the XAML designer, change the class name property to `MyStateMachine` as follows:

```
MyStateMachine.xaml*  + X  Program.cs*
<Activity mc:Ignorable="sap sap2010 sads"
          x:Class="WFStateMachine.MyStateMachine"
          sap2010:ExpressionActivityEditor.ExpressionActivityEditor="C#"
 xmlns="http://schemas.microsoft.com/netfx/2009/xaml/activities"
 xmlns:mc="http://schemas.openxmlformats.org/markup-compatibility/2006"
 xmlns:sads="http://schemas.microsoft.com/netfx/2010/xaml/activities/debugger"
 xmlns:sap="http://schemas.microsoft.com/netfx/2009/xaml/activities/presentation"
 xmlns:sap2010="http://schemas.microsoft.com/netfx/2010/xaml/activities/presentation"
 xmlns:sco="clr-namespace:System.Collections.ObjectModel;assembly=mscorlib"
 xmlns:x="http://schemas.microsoft.com/winfx/2006/xaml">
```

6. Note that we could perform this previous step on the designer by clicking on the canvas and pressing *F4* (properties), where we can set the x:Class value for the activity.

7. With this our project will be properly set up and we can proceed to creating our first .NET 4.5 state machine workflow.

   Close the XAML view of the WFStateMachine.xaml file and open it with a double-click or right-click on **View Designer**.

8. Lock the **Toolbox** pane and unfold the **StateMachine** section as follows:

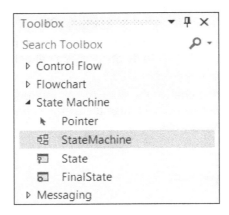

9. Drag-and-drop a **StateMachine** section at the center of the **MyStateMachine** designer. It should look similar to the following screenshot:

10. We will select the **StateMachine** blue canvas from the header, and on the **Properties** tab change the **DisplayName** property to `Book process StateMachine`.

11. In the section below the **StateMachine** section, click on the **Variables** button to unfold it and enter four variables, **NumberOfChapters**, **BookScore**, **ChapterScore**, and **SubmittedChapters**, of type **int32**. Make their scope the current activity so they look as shown in the following screenshot:

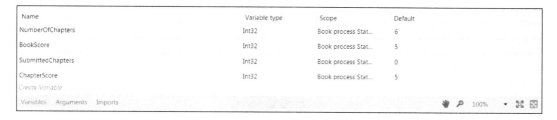

Name	Variable type	Scope	Default
NumberOfChapters	Int32	Book process Stat...	6
BookScore	Int32	Book process Stat...	5
SubmittedChapters	Int32	Book process Stat...	0
ChapterScore	Int32	Book process Stat...	5
Create Variable			

Variables Arguments Imports

12. In the **MyStateMachine** designer, we can observe the **Start** node and the first state. Change the first and only state by clicking on the name **State1** and change it to `Define Book`.

13. Move it just below the **Start** node and double-click on it to open it.

14. In the **Entry** section, add an **Assign** task from the **Toolbox** pane in the **Primitives** section as shown in the following screenshot:

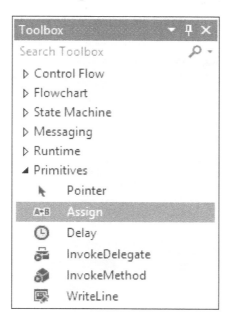

15. In the **To** section, add the **NumberOfChapters** variable name; we will observe that we have intelli-sense enabled, which will make our work easier.

16. In the **Enter a C# expression** box, we will enter `newSystem.Random().Next(4, 12)`. We could also type the expression directly in the **Properties** panel as follows:

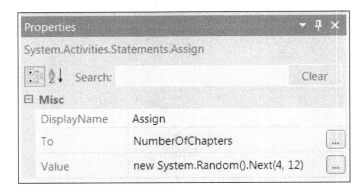

17. Next, select a **WriteLine** activity and drop it immediately below the **Assign** activity. While we are doing this, we should see a placeholder appearing. When we drop the new activity, we will see that the **Assign** and **WriteLine** activities have automatically been surrounded by another activity, a **Sequence** activity. This is what is called **auto surround with sequence**.

18. In the **Text** property of the **WriteLine** activity, add `"The book has been defined"`.

19. The **Define Book** state should now look as follows (do not worry about the **Transition(s)** section, we will add it in a few moments):

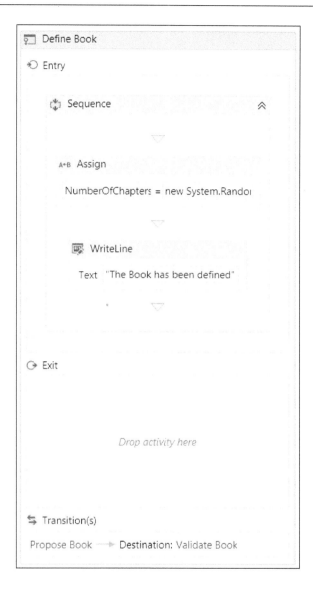

20. At the top we will see the navigation breadcrumb. We can click on the **Book process State Machine** link to go back and see the whole workflow.

21. We will add some more states to workflow: Validate Book, Create Chapter, Accept Chapter, Validate Chapter, and Process Chapter.

22. Additionally, we will add a Final state and place it at the bottom of the workflow.

23. We will now connect the states with transitions. To create a transition, move the cursor to the border of our first state **Define Book**; a square will appear, indicating that we can create a connector, that is dragging it to another state as follows:

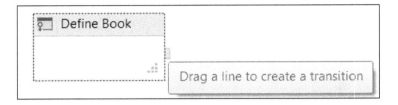

24. We will create a transition **Validate Book** by dragging this square into the **Validate Book** state.

25. Name it by selecting the transition (the line) and change the **DisplayName** value that appears on the **Properties** panel to Propose Book.

26. We will open the **Validate Book** activity and drop an **Assign** activity into its **Entry** section, after we set its **To** property to the **BookScore** variable and its value to the C# expression new System.Random().Next(1, 10).

27. From **Validate Book** we will create two transitions, one going back to the **Define Book** state and another to the **Create Chapter** state. We will name the first transition Book Denied and the second one Book Accepted.

28. Double-click on the **Book Denied** transition and enter the C# expression in the condition box as BookScore< 5.

29. In the **Action** section, drop a **WriteLine** activity and set its **Text** property to "Book has been denied..". It should now look like the following screenshot:

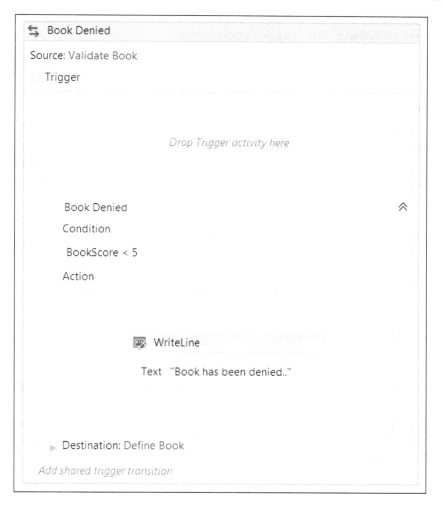

30. Click on the breadcrumb's **Book Process** state machine to go back to the general view of the workflow.

31. Double-click on the **Book Accepted** transition, set its condition to `BookScore>= 5`, and add a **WriteLine** activity with its **Text** property as `"Book has been accepted!"`.

32. In the **Create Chapter** state, we will add a **WriteLine** activity in its **Entry** section with the text `"We create/edit the chapter.."`. Next, add a **Delay** activity. On its **Properties** panel, we will set its duration to the expression `new TimeSpan(0,0,1)`.

33. In the **Create Chapter** section, we will create a transition called **Validate Chapter**, naming it `Submit for approval`.

34. On the **Submit for approval** transition, we will add a **WriteLine** activity with the text `"Submitting chapter for approval.."`.

35. Moving to our next state, that is, **Validate Chapter**, we will add a **WriteLine** activity with `"Validating Chapter.."` as its text.

36. Additionally, we will add an **Assign** task with the **ChapterScore** variable as its **To** parameter and `new System.Random().Next(1, 10)` as its value.

37. From this state, we will create two transitions, one to its previous state, **Create Chapter**, and another to the **Process Chapter** state, naming them `Chapter Denied` and `Chapter Accepted`, respectively.

38. For the **Chapter Denied** transition, include a condition `ChapterScore< 5` and add a **WriteLine** activity in the **Action** section, setting its text to `"The chapter has been denied.."`.

39. Give the **Chapter Accepted** transition a condition of `ChapterScore>= 5`, and in the **Action** section, add a **WriteLine** activity called the **Transaction** activity with the text set to `"The chapter has been accepted!"`.

40. In the **Entry** section in the **Process Chapter** state, add an **Assign** activity with **SubmittedChapters** as its **To** parameter and `SubmittedChapters = SubmittedChapters + 1` as its value.

41. From this **Process Chapter** state, we will create two transitions, one to the **Create Chapter** state named `Chapters Pending` and another to the **FinalState** state named `All Chapters Completed`.

42. On the **Chapters Pending** transition, we will add `SubmittedChapters<NumberOf Chapters` as its condition and a **WriteLine** activity on its **Action** panel with its **Text** property set to `"There are chapters to be finished"`.

43. For the **All Chapters Completed** transition, we will set its condition to `SubmittedChapters>= NumberOfChapters` and add a **WriteLine** activity on the **Action** panel with the **Text** set to `"All the chapters have been completed, congratulations!!"`.

44. In the **Final** state, we will add a **WriteLine** activity with the text `"You did it!"` and another **Delay** activity with the expression `new TimeSpan(0,0,5)` as its **Duration** parameter.

45. In order to facilitate testing, we will set a debug breakpoint by selecting the first state **Define Book** and pressing *F9*. To enter debug mode, press *F5* or click on the **Start debugging** button.

46. Observe that we can debug the whole workflow of the states and also their activities as follows:

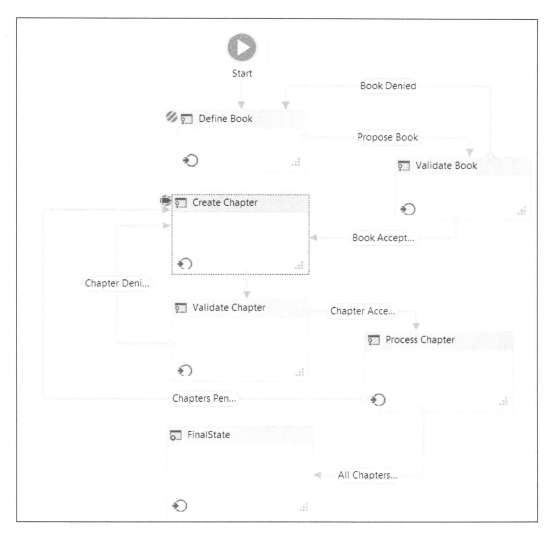

47. We can then watch the results through our **WriteLine** activities on the console as follows:

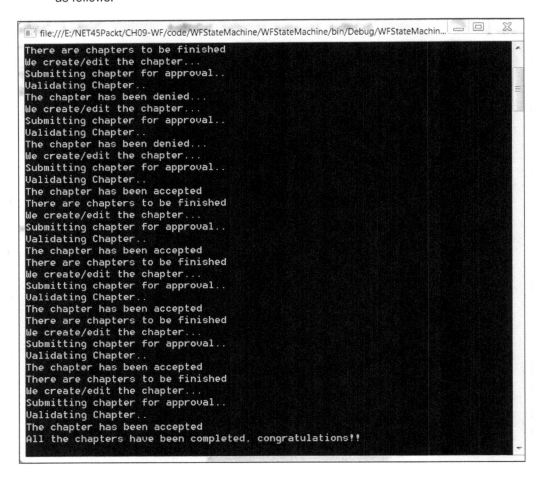

```
file:///E:/NET45Packt/CH09-WF/code/WFStateMachine/WFStateMachine/bin/Debug/WFStateMachin...

There are chapters to be finished
We create/edit the chapter...
Submitting chapter for approval..
Validating Chapter..
The chapter has been denied...
We create/edit the chapter...
Submitting chapter for approval..
Validating Chapter..
The chapter has been denied...
We create/edit the chapter...
Submitting chapter for approval..
Validating Chapter..
The chapter has been accepted
There are chapters to be finished
We create/edit the chapter...
Submitting chapter for approval..
Validating Chapter..
The chapter has been accepted
There are chapters to be finished
We create/edit the chapter...
Submitting chapter for approval..
Validating Chapter..
The chapter has been accepted
There are chapters to be finished
We create/edit the chapter...
Submitting chapter for approval..
Validating Chapter..
The chapter has been accepted
There are chapters to be finished
We create/edit the chapter...
Submitting chapter for approval..
Validating Chapter..
The chapter has been accepted
All the chapters have been completed, congratulations!!
```

Following the previous steps, we have successfully created a complete state machine workflow using some of the new capabilities of WF 4.5.

How it works...

We created a state machine workflow by adding a **StateMachine** activity and using it as a placeholder for our states and transitions, which we selected from the **StateMachine** section in our **Toolbox** pane.

We designed a book process workflow similar to the one used at Packt Publishing but much simpler. The preceding example showcases how to map a process to a workflow that is characterized by having fixed states and transitions between them.

The complete process needed a few more states and transitions to fulfill its intended behavior. We added activities on the state's entry points, but we could also have done so on the exit points.

The specific transition to use at each cycle is decided by examining the condition that we provided. For clarity and illustration purposes, we added a **WriteLine** activity to all the transitions so we could follow the execution in the console written out.

We have seen some examples of the usage of C# expressions, used the surround with a sequence capability of the improved designer, and used the bookmark to quickly navigate out of the transitions and states.

Finally, we debugged the workflow and saw how easy it has become with the new improvements.

Using the enhanced designer features

In this recipe, we will see how to use some of the new features of the workflow designer.

Enhanced designer features that we will be using include search, auto surround, panning, outline, and annotations.

Getting ready

In order to use this recipe, you should have Visual Studio 2012 installed. You need a project to work with, such as the result of our previous recipe.

How to do it...

We will explore some of the new WF designer features with the following steps:

1. First open Visual Studio 2012 and then open a WF 4.5 project. Our previous project will do perfectly.

2. Navigate from the menu to **View | Other windows | Document Outline** (or press *Ctrl + Alt + T*). The outline allows us to navigate with a simple click through the hierarchy of our workflow elements; this gives us a synchronized view of our workflow editor and our document outline, as we can see in the following screenshot:

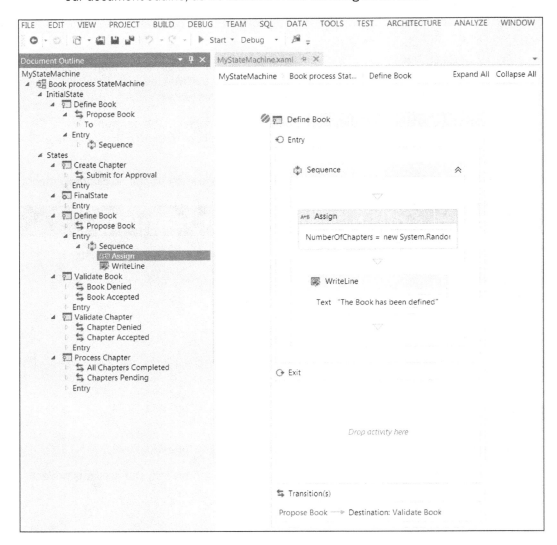

3. Press *Ctrl + F* to open the quick find **Find and Replace** dialog. Type `Validate` and click on the **Find Next** button. You can cycle through all the incidences of the word that have been found in your workflow.

4. Unfold the **Variables** panel and right-click on the topmost variable row. A context pop-up menu will appear with the **Delete** option, which already exists, that is used to perform operations with the keyboard.

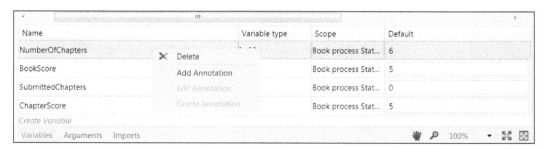

5. If you select three states while pressing the *Ctrl* key, they can then be jointly dragged. This enables us to multiselect and move states or activities on the designer (we previously had to make the selection one by one).

6. For complex workflows, we have the **Pan** mode. You can activate it by clicking on the hand at the bottom right of the workflow designer. We can simulate this by zooming in on our workflow so we can pan around.

7. On the state machine and in the flowchart workflows, we can drag a state on top of another state and see that both states become connected by a transition automatically. When dragging over the state, we will see that the attachment points become visible, indicating that when we drop the state. It will automatically get connected, as shown in the following screenshot. These features are called auto-connect and auto-insert.

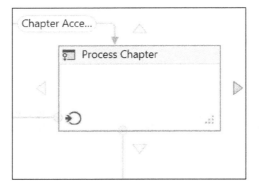

8. Right-click on the **Create Chapter** state and navigate to **Annotations | Add Annotation**. Enter `This is the step that will take most of the time...` If you now hover over the annotation icon at the top right of the step, the annotation will be shown. Note that you can collapse it so it will be displayed as a post-it note or expand it so it will be visible in the canvas.

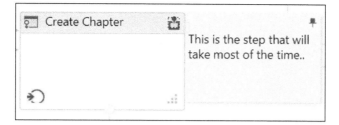

How it works...

We simply used the workflow designer on Visual Studio 2012 to showcase some of its new features.

We did not show the auto surround with sequence or the C# expressions, since we have already done so in the previous recipe. We also used the new debugger capabilities to debug the states and activities of a workflow.

A
Resources for Further Knowledge

In this chapter, we will cover:

- ▶ Resources for knowing more about .NET 4.5 and its tools
- ▶ Resources for knowing more about Windows 8
- ▶ Resources for knowing more about general development

Resources for knowing more about .NET 4.5 and its tools

Some resources of interest for .NET Framework 4.5 developers are as follows:

- ▶ The Visual Studio 2012 launch website `http://visualstudiolaunch.com/`.
- ▶ The .NET Framework blog `http://blogs.msdn.com/b/dotnet/`.
- ▶ The .NET Framework's Twitter handle `https://twitter.com/dotnet`.
- ▶ The Developer Tools Blogs `http://blogs.msdn.com/b/developer-tools/`.
- ▶ The Visual Studio Blogs `http://blogs.msdn.com/b/visualstudio/`.
- ▶ The Microsoft's Expression Blend team blog `http://blendinsider.com/`.
- ▶ The Visual Studio Developer Center `http://msdn.microsoft.com/visualstudio/`.
- ▶ The Visual Studio official website `http://www.microsoft.com/visualstudio`.

- The Visual Studio resources website `http://msdn.microsoft.com/vstudio`.
- Microsoft Developer Network's *What's New* in the .NET Framework 4.5 `http://msdn.microsoft.com/en-us/library/ms171868.aspx`.
- Microsoft's Virtual Academy `http://www.microsoftvirtualacademy.com/`.
- Microsoft's patterns and practices site `http://pnp.azurewebsites.net/en-us/`.
- Codeproject search for .NET 4.5 `http://www.codeproject.com/search.aspx?q=.net+4.5&x=-1287&y=-147&sbo=kw`.
- Channel 9 `http://channel9.msdn.com/`.
- The Microsoft Developer Network home website `http://msdn.microsoft.com/`.
- There is a really cool end-to-end sample, from being a web backend to a Windows Store app, that *Layla Driscoll* showcased at *TechEd North America* and *TechEd Europe*. It's called *What's New in the .NET Framework 4.5* and can be found at `http://code.msdn.microsoft.com/Whats-New-in-the-NET-e8d7545c`.

Resources for knowing more about Windows 8

Some cool resources for this outstanding platform, that is, Windows 8, are as follows:

- The event website where it all started: `http://www.buildwindows.com/`
- The section of the Microsoft Developer Network dedicated to the *Build* event where you can get any sessions you might have missed: `http://channel9.msdn.com/Events/BUILD/`
- The Windows 8 app developer blog: `http://blogs.msdn.com/b/windowsappdev/`
- The Windows dev center: `http://msdn.microsoft.com/en-US/windows`
- The Windows Store apps developer center: `http://msdn.microsoft.com/en-us/windows/apps`
- Developer downloads for creating Windows Store apps: `http://msdn.microsoft.com/en-US/windows/apps/br229516.aspx`
- The Windows Store apps samples: `http://code.msdn.microsoft.com/windowsapps/`
- If you are interested in Windows 8, you might want to attend a Windows 8 Dev Camp: `http://www.devcamps.ms/windows`

    If you cannot attend, check *"The Contoso Cookbook App" Hands-on-Lab*; it is simply great!

- ▸ Download *"The Contoso Cookbook App" Hands-on-Lab* from `http://www.microsoft.com/en-us/download/details.aspx?id=29854`

- ▸ You can work with the hands-on-lab through the virtual labs platform available at `http://msdn.microsoft.com/en-us/jj206431.aspx`

- ▸ Of course, Windows 8 wouldn't be the same without one of the best, if not the best, frameworks for MVVM development, MVVM Light, which you can grab from `http://mvvmlight.codeplex.com/`

- ▸ Laurent Bugnion's blog also has an interesting post related to Windows 8 development at `http://blog.galasoft.ch/`

- ▸ Additionally, you will find some interesting posts about Windows 8 in my blog `http://silverlightguy.com`

Resources for knowing more about general development

Finally, some interesting resources for a few areas specific to .NET 4.5 development are as follows:

- ▸ The Base Class Library (BCL) blog: `http://blogs.msdn.com/b/bclteam/`

- ▸ The Parallel Programming with .NET blog: `http://blogs.msdn.com/b/pfxteam/`

- ▸ The ADO.NET (Entity Framework too) blog: `http://blogs.msdn.com/b/adonet/`

- ▸ The Data Developer Center: `http://msdn.microsoft.com/en-us/data`

- ▸ The ASP.NET website: `http://www.asp.net/`

- ▸ The ASP.NET Web API (inside the ASP.NET website): `http://www.asp.net/web-api`

- ▸ The Windows Client website, `http://windowsclient.net/`, which contains resources for WPF (Windows Presentation Foundation) and Windows Forms

.NET 4.5 – Deployment Risks and Issues

In this appendix, I will expose some deployment risks and issues that might occur with .NET 4.5.

Introduction

As mentioned in *Chapter 2, Exploring the Top New Features of the CLR*, .NET 4.5 is an *in-place* replacement for .NET 4.0, which only runs on Windows Vista SP2 or later systems.

This means that when .NET 4.5 is installed, it replaces the .NET 4.0 assemblies; even though .NET 4.5 has very high compatibility with .NET 4.0 scenarios, it might behave differently.

This comes along with the possibility that one of the deployment targets might not be supported by .NET 4.5, such as Windows XP.

Along the same lines, we can install Visual Studio 2012 in our machine along with Visual Studio 2010; they can be run side by side.

Next we will see these points and their risks in some detail, specifically mentioning the following:

- Risks of the in-place upgrade to .NET 4.5
- Platform targeting

Additionally, we will expose some risk points to keep in mind while developing with the .NET 4.5 framework.

Risks of the in-place upgrade

When .NET 4.5 is installed, it effectively replaces the existing .NET 4.0 assemblies in the machine; they are overwritten by a newer version.

Curiously, when we query the runtime version, `Environment.Version` is still 4.0.30319, having differences only in the build numbers. Basically, it becomes hard for the application to identify if we are running .NET 4.0 or 4.5, which might be necessary if we have to decide which part of the code can or cannot be executed.

And yes, we can build an application on .NET 4.5 and execute it on .NET 4.0, but these might not run properly if it uses some features of the .NET 4.5 framework. Otherwise, building .NET 4.0 applications with .NET 4.5 should not bring any problems.

For avoiding these issues, we should use the `<supportedruntime>` element, which specifies the versions of the CLR supported by the application with a syntax like the following:

```
<supportedRuntime version="runtime version" sku="sku id"/>
```

If this is not found on the application configuration file, the runtime version used to build the application will be used. An example of this configuration is the following:

```
<configuration>
    <startup>
        <supportedRuntime version="v4.0" sku=".
NETFramework,Version=v4.5" />
    </startup>
</configuration>
```

With this in place, the application will know that it needs .NET 4.5; if it is not installed, our application will not run and propose to install it.

Note that most of the client applications add this automatically, but we must keep an eye out for it or we might be surprised.

Platform targeting

A .NET 4.5 application will not run on an unsupported platform such as Windows XP.

We must have in mind which operating systems support .NET 4.5. At the time of writing this book, they were:

- Windows 8
- Windows 7

- ▶ Windows Vista SP2
- ▶ Windows Server 2012
- ▶ Windows Server 2008 R2
- ▶ Windows Server 2008 SP2

Other risks

We might have to consider other risks as well, as follows:

- ▶ The performance improvements and bug fixes of .NET 4.5 might help pass some tests if run on .NET 4.5, but they will not in .NET 4.0. An application can run perfectly over .NET 4.5 and have errors running on .NET 4.0. Note that, for this to happen, it must target .NET 4.0. An example of this is saving an enum value in the LINQ 2 entities; this will work perfectly in .NET 4.5, but will provoke an error on a machine with .NET 4.0.

- ▶ In a development team, a developer installing Visual Studio 2012 will install and replace its assemblies with .NET 4.5, running the risk of modifying the project and/or its behavior. His installation might also produce different execution behavior than his peers.

Index

Symbols

-Force flag 86
.NET 4.5
 about 67
 deployment risks 203
 features 67
 issues 203
 new features 117, 118
 platforms 204
 resources 199
 RESTful applications 161
 risks 205
-Script flag 87

A

AddColumn function 86
Add-Migration command 87
application
 improving, toast notifications adding 40, 41
application domain default culture
 defining 52, 53
application tile
 improving 33-39
Application UI tab 41
ASP.NET 89, 90
ASP.NET MVC4 161
ASP.NET web API
 creating 162-169
 support 162
 working 169, 170
ASP.NET Web Forms application
 creating 90-103
async
 about 59
 using 59-63

asynchronous error handling
 implementing, INotifyDataErrorInfo
  used 118-124
asynchronous features, WCF
 using 145-149
asynchronous HTTP module
 about 114
 creating 114-116
auto surround with sequence 186
await
 about 59
 using 59-63

B

Base Class Library. *See* **BCL**
BCL 9
BindData() method 142
BooksModel class 120
BooksModel.cs class 179

C

CancellationToken method 129
CheckPreviousExecution() method 29
Code First application
 complex types 83
 Connection string 83
 creating 76-84
 Primary key 83
 Relationship 83
 Typediscovery 83
 working 82, 83
Code First Migrations
 about 84
 using 84-87

CodePlex state machine 181
constructor method 25
Contract First 182
Contract First development
  about 156
  using 156-158
  working 159
Controller... option 164
CopyFilesWithFileStreams method 64
CopyFolderContents() method 66
Create Read Update and Delete. *See* CRUD
CRUD 170
CRUD ASP.NET web API
  implementing 170-174
  working 174
CustomReflectionContext class 53

D

data
  binding, to static properties 130-132
data source
  update delays, throttling 133-137
DbContext class 82
DEBUG button 168
default reflection behavior
  overriding 53-55
DefineAppDomainCulture() method 52
Directory.EnumerateFiles method 66
Dispatcher.Invoke method 129
dispatcher's new features
  using 127-129
dispose method 115
DropCreateDatabaseIfModelChanges
      base 101

E

EAI 67
EF 75
E-mail Address Internationalization. *See* EAI
Enable-Migrations command 87
enhanced designer features
  about 193
  using 193-197
Entity Framework. *See* EF
EventHandlerTaskAsyncHelper class 116

Extract to User Control feature
  using 111, 112

F

first Windows Store app
  building 10-18
  splash screen, adding 21
  working 19-21

G

general development
  resources 201
general development, resources
  ADO.NET (Entity Framework too) blog 201
  ASP.NET Web API 201
  ASP.NET website 201
  BCL (Base Class Library) blog 201
  Data Developer Center 201
  Parallel Programming with .NET blog 201
  Windows Client website 201
GenerateBooks() method 170
GetAsync method 72
GetBookCategories() method 112
GetURLContentsAsync method 62

H

HTML editor
  Smart Tasks, using 107, 109
HttpClient
  about 68
  using 68-72
  working 72-74
HttpResponseMessage class 72
HttpResponseMessage method 73
HttpTestAsync function 60
HttpTestAsync method 62

I

IDN 67
IETF 67
Initializer class 92
INotifyDataErrorInfo
  used, for asynchronous error handling imple-
      mentation 118-124

in-place upgrade
  risks 204
Internationalized Domain Name. *See* **IDN**
Internet Engineering Task Force. *See* **IETF**
IoC 162
IsOnSale property 85

L

Launch Toast button 41
LiveShaping
  about 138
  steps 138-142

M

MainWindow.xaml class 135, 141
Managed Extensibility Framework. *See* **MEF**
MEF 44
Model-View-ViewModel. *See* **MVVM**
Multicore JIT 44
MVVM 8
MyAppBindableData property 26

N

new asynchronous file I/O operations
  using 63-66
  working 66
new ZipArchive class
  using 56-59
NotifyPropertyChanged event 133

O

OData 162
OnActivated event 27
OnActivated method 32
OnLaunched method 27, 32, 35
OnModelCreating method 83

P

Page Inspector feature
  about 112
  using 113
  working 114

Pan mode 196
Pixel option 16
portable library
  about 45
  creating 45-48
  working 48, 49
PrepareMessage method 26

R

RegEx.IsMatch() method 51
regular expression timeout
  controlling 49, 50
  working 51
RemoveHandler method 127
resources, .NET 4.5 199, 200
resources, Windows 8 200
RESTful applications 161
risks, .NET 4.5 205

S

SaveUserSessionData method 26
SaveUserSessionData() method 31
self-hosted ASP.NET web API
  about 175
  setting up 175-179
ShowAttributes method 54
side versioning 182
Smart Tasks
  using, in HTML editor 107-109
splash screen
  adding, to Windows Store app 21-23
StartSendingData() method 155
StartUpdatingData() method 143
state machine workflow
  about 182
  creating 183-193
static properties
  data, binding to 130-132
StaticPropertyChanged event 132
svcutil tool 159
System.Net.Http namespaces
  about 68
  using 68-72
  working 72-74

T

Task-Based Asynchronous Pattern 149
Task Parallel Library. *See* **TPL**
Task.WhenAll() method 149
Text property 131
throttling 137
TPL 44

U

Uniform Resource Identifier. *See* **URI**
unobtrusive validation
  using, by application configuration 103, 106
Update-Database command 86, 87
update delays, data source
  throttling 133-138
URI 67
user experience (UX) 24

W

WAI-ARIA
  about 109
  using 109
WCF
  asynchronous features 145-149
WCF 4.5 145
WeakEventManager
  using, with WeakEvent pattern 125, 126
WeakEventManager class 126

WeakEvent pattern
  using, with WeakEventManager 125, 126
Web Accessibility Initiative-Accessible Rich Internet Applications. *See* **WAI-ARIA**
WebClient method 115
WebSockets
  about 149
  using 149-154
  working 154, 155
WF 181
Windows 8
  resources 200, 201
Windows Presentation Foundation. *See* **WPF**
Windows Push Notification Services. *See* **WNS**
Windows Store apps
  about 7-9
  complying, with Windows 8 lifecycle
    model 24-33
  principles 9
  programming model 8
WNS 40, 42
Workflow Foundation. *See* **WF**
WPF 9, 117
WriteLine activity 193

X

XmlDocument variable 38

Thank you for buying
Microsoft .NET Framework 4.5 Quickstart Cookbook

About Packt Publishing

Packt, pronounced 'packed', published its first book "*Mastering phpMyAdmin for Effective MySQL Management*" in April 2004 and subsequently continued to specialize in publishing highly focused books on specific technologies and solutions.

Our books and publications share the experiences of your fellow IT professionals in adapting and customizing today's systems, applications, and frameworks. Our solution-based books give you the knowledge and power to customize the software and technologies you're using to get the job done. Packt books are more specific and less general than the IT books you have seen in the past. Our unique business model allows us to bring you more focused information, giving you more of what you need to know, and less of what you don't.

Packt is a modern, yet unique publishing company, which focuses on producing quality, cutting-edge books for communities of developers, administrators, and newbies alike. For more information, please visit our website: www.PacktPub.com.

About Packt Enterprise

In 2010, Packt launched two new brands, Packt Enterprise and Packt Open Source, in order to continue its focus on specialization. This book is part of the Packt Enterprise brand, home to books published on enterprise software – software created by major vendors, including (but not limited to) IBM, Microsoft and Oracle, often for use in other corporations. Its titles will offer information relevant to a range of users of this software, including administrators, developers, architects, and end users.

Writing for Packt

We welcome all inquiries from people who are interested in authoring. Book proposals should be sent to author@packtpub.com. If your book idea is still at an early stage and you would like to discuss it first before writing a formal book proposal, contact us; one of our commissioning editors will get in touch with you.

We're not just looking for published authors; if you have strong technical skills but no writing experience, our experienced editors can help you develop a writing career, or simply get some additional reward for your expertise.

Ext.NET Web Application
Development

A guide to building Rich Internet Applications with Ext.NET using ASP.NET Web Forms and ASP.NET MVC

Anup Shah

Ext.NET Web Application Development

ISBN: 978-1-849693-24-0   Paperback: 410 pages

A guide to building Rich Internet Applications with Ext.NET using ASP.NET Web Forms and ASP.NET MVC

1. Build rich internet applications using the power of Ext.NET controls

2. Learn how Ext.NET leverages Sencha's popular Ext JS JavaScript framework to provide a full client-server web development experience

3. Full of examples and tips, with clear step-by-step instructions

Learn by doing: less theory, more results

.NET 4.0 Generics

Enhance the type safety of your code and create applications easily using Generics in .NET Framework 4.0

Foreword by
Dr. Don Syme, Principal Researcher, Microsoft Research, Cambridge, U.K.
Dr. Andrew Kennedy, Researcher, Microsoft Research, Cambridge, U.K.

Beginner's Guide

Sudipta Mukherjee

.NET 4.0 Generics Beginner's Guide

ISBN: 978-1-849690-78-2   Paperback: 396 pages

Enhance the type safety of your code and create applications easily using Generics in .NET Framework 4.0

1. Learn how to use Generics' methods and generic collections to solve complicated problems.

2. Develop real-world applications using Generics

3. Know the importance of each generic collection and Generic class and use them as per your requirements

Please check **www.PacktPub.com** for information on our titles

WCF 4.5 Multi-Layer Services Development with Entity Framework

ISBN: 978-1-849687-66-9   Paperback: 394 pages

Build SOA applications on Microsoft platforms with this hands-on guide

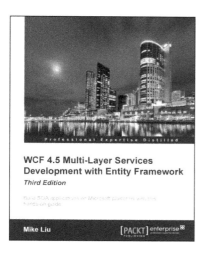

WCF 4.5 Multi-Layer Services Development with Entity Framework
Third Edition

Build SOA applications on Microsoft platforms with this hands-on guide

Mike Liu

1. This book will teach you WCF, Entity Framework, LINQ, and LINQ to Entities quickly and easily.

2. Apply best practices to your WCF services and utilize Entity Framework in your WCF services.

3. Practical, with step-by-step instructions and precise screenshots, this is a truly hands-on book for all C++, C#, and VB.NET developers.

Microsoft Visual Studio LightSwitch Business Application Development

ISBN: 978-1-849682-86-2   Paperback: 384 pages

A jump-start guide to application development with Microsoft's Visual Studio LightSwitch

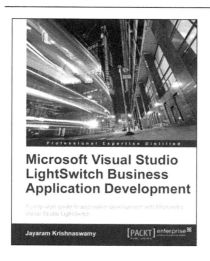

Microsoft Visual Studio LightSwitch Business Application Development

A jump-start guide to application development with Microsoft's Visual Studio LightSwitch

Jayaram Krishnaswamy

1. Easily connect to various data sources with practical examples and easy-to-follow instructions

2. Create entities and screens both from scratch and using built-in templates

3. Query using built-in designer and by coding (both VB and C#)

Please check **www.PacktPub.com** for information on our titles

www.ingramcontent.com/pod-product-compliance
Lightning Source LLC
Chambersburg PA
CBHW060552060326
40690CB00017B/3684